GRAPPLE WITH GUILT, SHED THE SHAME

Getting Over Your Past & On With Your Life

Sheila M. Luck

An Elizabeth Ministry International Resource
120 W. 8th Street, Kaukauna, WI
www.elizabethministry.com

Unless otherwise indicated, all Scripture quotations are from the *Life Application Study Bible,* New International Version®, co-published by Tyndale House Publisher, Inc., Wheaton IL, and Zondervan Publishing House, Grand Rapids, MI, Copyright © 1988, 1989, 1990 and 1991. The Bible text used in this edition of the Life Application Study Bible is the Holy Bible, New International Version®, copyright 1973, 1978, and 1984 by International Bible Society. *All rights reserved.*

Scripture quotations marked (NLT) are taken from the Holy Bible, New Living Translation, Copyright 1996. Used by permission of Tyndale House Publishers, Inc., Wheaton, IL 60189. *All rights reserved.*

Copyright © 2007 Sheila M. Luck; modified and reprinted by The Life & Loss Institute, Inc., D.B.A. Elizabeth Ministry International, Inc., © 2013 Sheila M. Luck/The Life & Loss Institute, Inc.

Cover photo Copyright © 2012 Krista M. Luck, N5821 Gilman Road, Scandinavia, WI 54977. Used with permission.

All rights reserved. No part of this publication may be reproduced, stored in a retrieval system, or transmitted in any form or by any means–electronic, mechanical, photocopy, recording, or any other–except for brief quotations in printed or digital reviews without the prior written permission of the publisher.

Printed and Manufactured in the United States of America

Important Note: If at any time you feel you need to speak with a pastoral or professional Christian counselor, please call your church office for a referral to a member of their pastoral staff or a licensed professional Christian counselor.

Dedication

I commit this work unto the Lord.
May all who work through this Bible study know
God is love, and
God loves you.

Acknowledgments

Knowing how busy one's life can be, I have never wanted to impose on others' time. Afraid that asking for help or advice would put someone on the spot or burden them in a very unwanted way, I have spent a lifetime avoiding asking others for help. (Perhaps my sense of shame prevented me from asking for help.) However, far from being an expert on this topic, I knew that the only possible way for me to complete this work with wisdom, knowledge, breadth and compassion was through the help of many others and, of course, lots and lots of prayer.

So I asked for help. I asked and asked. The amazing willingness of others to help at all turns never ceases to amaze me! I thank you all!

First, I thank all of the friends, relatives, and newly found friends, most of whom will remain nameless to protect the promised anonymity, for sharing their many stories of guilt and often burdensome shame. Some stories were humorous, some were painful, and others wore heavy on the heart. Some stories were from the distant past, while others are on-going today. Some situations remembered created laughter, while many brought forth tears. For many, the wounds have healed. But for others, there is regret, anger, hatred, sadness, lost love, or bitterness. I thank you for sharing your stories with me. I pray that through your stories, this Bible study might reach the hearts of many other people and help them take the first step toward healing.

I thank my daughters, both of whom I am so proud. They have both consistently done their best in school. They don't drink, smoke or do drugs. They have a solid group of friends that are on healthy, God-loving paths. They respect those in authority and honor their parents. (I'm not making this up!) When I asked them if they had any guilt or shame stories to share, one daughter laughed. The other daughter jokingly fabricated an outlandish tale. I thank them for choosing to walk closely with God. Through them, I have observed the joy and peace that comes from a life that is based in God's love, a life without toxic shame.

I thank my husband. He knows my struggles with the shame of my past choices. Yet, he provided the earthly love and support that I needed to begin to overcome such struggles. He walked with me along my faith journey, the ultimate path toward Jesus Christ, from whom I got the strength to conquer the affects of unresolved guilt and resultant shame.

Finally, I thank my friend, Colleen Hansen, and my cousin, Pastor Vilas Mazemke, for taking the time to read, review and critique this work. Their help was essential for the overall quality of this work.

For each and every one of you, and for all that read this Bible study, I pray:

May the Lord bless you

and keep you;

May the Lord make his face shine upon you

and be gracious to you;

May the Lord turn his face toward you

and give you peace. (From Numbers 6:24-26)

Contents

Using This Workbook 11
Introduction: Guilt and Shame 15
Author's Story: Now I Live in Peace! 21
Your Story: Shame is Everywhere 27
Week 1: I'm Exhausted! 31
Week 2: Why Would God Help Me? 47
Week 3: If Only I Had... 57
Week 4: Grappling with Guilt 69
Week 5: I Confess, I Repent 83
Week 6: I Am Forgiven! 95
Week 7: But I'm Angry! 109
Week 8: Jesus Knows Your Pain 123
Week 9: I Didn't Do It 137
Week 10: I Shed the Shame 151
References 165
Memory Verses 167

Using This Workbook

For many years, psychological studies focused on the myriad of emotions, feelings or issues prevalent in society, including things like anger, hatred, love, rage, self-worth and more. However, the impact of guilt and shame was not widely studied or analyzed until sometime in the 1980s. Today, there are many books and articles written on the topics of guilt and shame, some emphasizing guilt and shame as stand alone topics, and some showing how guilt or shame may be an underlying cause of another emotional or psychological problem, such as depression. The books and articles cover the wide range of the sources of guilt and shame as well as the wide range of ways that guilt and shame might manifest in a person's behaviors. Many of these are listed on the References page in the back of this book.

Some resources use the terms guilt and shame differently than other resources.

With that in mind, we will start with a definition of guilt and shame as these terms are used in this workbook; we will learn how guilt or shame might impact one's life; and we will briefly identify many of the common sources for shame in our lives. Then throughout the weekly Bible study, we will learn to identify the source of shame, accept responsibility for our own guilt and resultant shame, appropriately recognize when that responsibility lies with someone else, and study the biblical paths which open the doors toward healthy management and healing of the guilt or shame that may be adversely impacting our lives.

This workbook is designed to be completed within ten weekly meetings. However, if the group is able to schedule twelve meetings, I encourage you to do so. The first week would then be devoted to reading the introductory materials, and getting to know each other a little better. The last week would be reserved for schedule slippage, allowing for extra time in any one or more meetings so that the group does not need to rush if you are in the middle of a meaningful conversation.

If you schedule ten meetings for your group, each participant is encouraged to read the introductory materials and my personal story in the beginning of the workbook prior to the first meeting.

If you are using this workbook on your own, do not worry. A group leader is not necessary to understand and to work through the content.

Within each week's materials, I describe additional stories involving some form of guilt or shame. Most of these were obtained by interviewing friends, relatives, and acquaintances, as well as a couple additional experiences of my own and a few fictional compilations of stories I have read or with which I have otherwise become familiar. These stories are intended to first illustrate the many faces and sources of guilt or shame, and second to serve as a backdrop for the week's Bible study.

After the weekly stories and related discussion questions, you will find a short Bible study intended to help each participant relate God's Word to the subjects to be discussed for the week. I pray that you will find avenues for God's peace through his Word.

At the end of each weekly section, there are suggested homework activities. These will enable you to dig more deeply into your personal experiences in the privacy of your home. Then during each subsequent week, you will be given the opportunity to share with the others in the group what you may have learned through the homework exercises. Such sharing is optional, of course.

From time to time, you might find the discussion too painful for your active participation. It is okay to silently listen, reflect, and pray. But I encourage you to share your struggles with each other. Remember, you are not alone in your shame. Allow God to lead you. Allow him to open your heart, your mind, and your memory. The path may be difficult at times, but trust him to be with you on every step.

I believe that everyone can and should be encouraged and supported through the understanding and compassion of other people, particularly those that have faced similar circumstances. Encouraging one another is a natural part of

> From time to time, you might find the discussion too painful for your active participation. It is okay to silently listen, reflect, and pray.

God's plan. However, for some of you, once the doors to your past have been opened, you may find that you feel deep sadness, depression, or maybe even worse. If you have symptoms that are debilitating, seriously harmful to your health or well-being, or interfering with your ability to work or manage your daily activities, I urge you to seek help from a pastoral or professional Christian counselor. Please call your church office for a referral to an appropriate member of the pastoral staff or to a licensed professional Christian counselor. Remember that I am not a professional counselor. Although I have written this workbook based in part on my own personal recovery from shame, coupled with extensive research on the subject, neither my words nor this Bible study should be used in place of quality, professional counseling when needed.

I am not a stranger to the topics of guilt and shame. After years of walking independently and trying to carry the shameful emotions from my past mistakes alone, I finally sought God's helping hand. Through him, I have found peace. For the most part, I believe I have shed the shame that has followed me for most of my adult years. Healing from shame is not usually a fast process, and it often includes painful memories or personal reflections. I pray that you, too, will find hope and peace.

If you want to pursue additional reading or other resources, I encourage you to consider some of the resources noted on the References section in the back of this book.

> So there is hope for your future, declares the Lord.
> Jeremiah 31:17

Overview

Guilt and Shame

what are they?

What is guilt? What is shame? Are they the same thing? Are they different? Do they overlap? Is guilt a subset of shame?

Experts have defined these terms a little differently in attempt to create clarity in their writings. Some experts have limited the use of the word guilt to the technical issue of whether we are guilty of wrongdoing, and then used shame to define our subsequent feelings. They explain that guilty feelings are a subset of shame. Then they differentiate between healthy shame (feelings which guide our behaviors or encourage us to make personal changes in our lives) and toxic shame (feelings of disgrace, dislike, or hatred that we direct at ourselves, defining ourselves as worthless or unworthy). (See, for example, the writings by Drs. Daniel Green and Mel Lawrenz listed in the References section of page 165).

Other experts have defined the word guilt as the feeling of regret or remorse over something a person has done. Used in this way, guilt is the feeling generated by our conscience which ultimately tells us to do or not to do something. Guilt then is a feeling directed toward our actions, activities, things we have done, or things we have failed to do. When we feel guilt, we might say or think things like, "I shouldn't have done that. Why did I do that? I knew it was wrong before I did it, yet I did it anyway. I made a huge mistake. I wish I hadn't hurt her feelings." (See, for example, the writings by Rev. Paul A. Feider listed in the References section of page 165).

These same experts then use the term shame to reflect negative feelings directed at ourselves rather than at our actions. If we feel shame, we might say or think things like, "I'm so stupid. How come I can never do anything right? I'm just dirt.

No one could possibly love me. I don't deserve to be treated with respect."

Shame finds fault with the person, and guilt finds fault with the action.

It can be confusing. Because we often think of our feelings that relate to something that we have done as guilty feelings, I will use the term guilt in this workbook when I am talking about the way we feel about something we have done or not done. I will use the term shame when I am talking about the way we feel about ourselves, whether those feelings have evolved from something we have done or from some other source.

Grappling with our guilt is a healthy and necessary step for both individual and societal well-being. We grapple with our guilt by correcting our behaviors or by making amends for the wrongs that we have done. If we have done something wrong, we can often manage and ultimately resolve our feelings of guilt through confession, restitution, reconciliation and correction. However, occasionally, because some wrongdoings have consequences that cannot be fixed or eliminated, it may be difficult or seemingly impossible to resolve our feelings of guilt. Unresolved guilty feelings often lead to feelings of shame, feelings of worthlessness or unworthiness or unacceptability that may be difficult to shed.

Sometimes we develop feelings of guilt and ultimately shame because we simply think we did something wrong. For example, we may dwell inordinately on the "what ifs" and "should haves" in life. We might say things like, "I should have taken that other job because my family would have been better off. I should have called her while she was in the hospital to let her know that I cared about her. I should have said something before it was too late. I shouldn't have let him take the car that night." Our feelings related to the "should haves" in life are feelings of guilt, in that we wonder if we could have made better choices. Inordinately dwelling on these things may convince us that we are foolish, less than adequate, or stupid. The feelings of guilt have then evolved into feelings of shame.

Some people, usually for those that already have a sense of personal shame, leap directly to feelings of shame when they begin to experience feelings of guilt due to something that they have done wrong, or something they think they have done wrong. As a result, often the smallest wrongdoing may cause some people to slip deeper into their sense of shame.

As discussed, shame may result from our guilty feelings about an actual or perceived wrongdoing. However, shame can develop in several other ways. It may be self-imposed as a result of things that have happened to us or around us, or it may be imposed upon us by the wrongdoings of others or by the actions of an entire community, or it may be shame that we have adopted as our own, which in fact belongs to another person.

For example, we may feel shame as a result of a job loss due to a company downsizing or rightsizing. In past years, corporations in America have forced thousands of people to leave what they thought were successful jobs with long-term futures, at no fault of their own. Many people struggle with such loss, feeling embarrassment, self-doubt, and ultimately shame. This shame is self-imposed as the result of the surrounding circumstances. In fact, in this example, there was no wrongdoing by anyone.

Shame may be imposed upon us by the wrongdoings of another person. The shame may be the result of regular, repeated, and undeserved attacks on one's work skills by an ungrateful boss or a jealous co-worker. Others have faced abuse such as rape or incest or physical beatings. Some people may have had a parent that was emotionally abusive. For example, a parent might repeatedly tell her children that they are stupid or "good for nothing." Other parents will withhold praise out of the mistaken idea that if the children are praised, they won't try as hard next time. Some parents set unrealistic expectations for their children and harshly chastise or punish them when they fail to live up to those expectations. Spouses are often abusive to each other. A husband may repeatedly criticize his wife for making mistakes, failing to keep the house clean, or letting the kids "dress in rags." Women, too, have been known to emotionally abuse their husbands through endless criticism of their jobs, income level, clothing, or abilities as a father or as head of the household.

Shame might also be imposed on us by the society or community in which we live or by a group within our society. Racial intolerance, bullying, "losing face," and shunning are ways that shame is imposed by a particular societal circle. For example, an individual may simply be excluded from his peer group. This might happen at a place of employment, where all co-workers ignore, exclude or belittle a particular co-worker. It is a relatively common occurrence among school children or teens when the main group belittles, teases or harasses someone that is deemed different or less popular. It can even happen within families, when one sibling is singled out by the others and then repeatedly mistreated either physically or emotionally. As a final example, negative gossip within a small town, community or organization may impose shame on the person that is the subject of the gossip.

Finally, adopted shame is often based on a sense of responsibility for or humiliation over the actions of someone close to us. For example, we might feel shame as the result of a parent's alcoholism, a spouse's drug addiction, or an adult child's criminal activity. It is not uncommon for children of divorced parents to believe they caused the divorce by not behaving well, by not being sufficiently lovable, or by some other false notion. These beliefs can turn into intense feelings of shame even though the person feeling the shame held no actual responsibility for the situation. The person adopts the feelings of shame that rightly belong elsewhere. In essence, we take responsibility for the wrongdoings or unfortunate circumstances of another, even though we had no control over the situation.

Shame can be healthy, in that there may be something about ourselves that we should try to improve or correct. However, shame may also be toxic.

Toxic shame manifests itself in many forms. It may be the root cause for feelings of insecurity, lack of self-confidence, depression, humiliation, helplessness, weakness, shyness, and low self-esteem. It might be the basis for a variety of negative behaviors involving issues such as an inability to say no, an inability to make decisions, procrastination, underachieving, self-condemnation, self-criticism, withdrawal from other people or social settings, and self-destructive behaviors. Self-destructive behaviors include excessive spending, eating disorders, alcohol abuse, drug abuse, sexual addictions, and self-mutilation. Often, seemingly positive behaviors can also be based in shame, particularly if the person practices these behaviors in excess. These include perfectionism, overachieving, over-working, domineering leadership, over-pleasing, and self-sacrificing.

I have lived a lifetime grappling with guilt and trying to shed my shame. In telling about one aspect of my life related to my crisis pregnancy at age seventeen, I will try to show the

> He who keeps the law is a discerning son, but a companion of gluttons disgraces his father.
> Proverbs 28:7

pervasive impact of guilt and shame. At the same time, I want to leave you with a sense of hope. At some point in our lives, we will all grapple with our guilt. At some point, many of us will want to shed our shame.

Author's Story

Now I Live in Peace!

freedom from guilt

*Note:
It is anticipated that this section will be read by the group participants on their own time.*

How do I explain it? I wallowed in it for so many years. Shame. It seemed to be a permanent part of me, but now it is gone. I've shed the shame of my past choices, the choices that seemed to follow me wherever I went and tainted everything I did and everything I tried to be.

I've shed the shame.

I live in peace.

Shedding the shame and finding peace does not mean that I have now concluded that I made correct choices when I was seventeen years old. It does not mean that I no longer care about the impact of my choices. It also does not mean that the forever and ever consequences of my choices are resolved. It doesn't mean that I no longer look back on my ultimate decision with sorrow. It doesn't mean that I never have feelings of grief and regret for choosing abortion.

What it means is that the burden of unresolved guilt and the resultant shame is gone. It means no more and it means no less. The shame that was such a heavy burden to carry has been lifted from my soul. I can now stop denying or justifying the ultimate choice. I can stop hiding it and running from it. I can stop trying to prove my worth.

The choice to have an abortion when I was seventeen was what I believed to be the only available choice at the time. It was the choice of a desperate teenager with perceived limited options, facing what I believed would be a life of shame and community ridicule for getting pregnant, for getting caught, and for not living up to the standards expected of me. I believed that I was facing a future with no home to call my own, no family support, no money, no opportunity for better education or employment, and no love. I feared the community gossip, the loss of friends, the loss of my family, and the expected loneliness.

I ran from my fears. I felt guilty about having an intimate relationship without being married. I felt guilty when I discovered I was pregnant. I feared the shame of facing my family, my friends and the people in my community. I feared their gossip, their anger, and their lack of compassion. At the time, I thought the choice to have an abortion saved me from my fear of certain shame.

I didn't know at the time that running from my immediate fears would only lead to another source of guilt and ultimately shame. In fact, at first, I felt relief following the abortion. The one person that knew of the abortion at the time said that he could almost see the weight of my fears lifting from my shoulders. He could see my relief. He could see then how I believed that I had fully resolved my problem, and I could now move forward in life without facing my guilt for becoming pregnant, and the shame that would be imposed upon me by all who found out.

I went on with life, putting the decision behind me, hiding my pregnancy and my ultimate choice from everyone. I told no one. When confronted with the truth, I lied.

It worked. I had a new future. Or so I thought. I didn't understand the truth. I hadn't yet realized the impact of my choice.

At the time of the abortion, I believed that my body was simply preparing tissue for the baby that would soon begin to grow. I had never pictured a baby, at least not up to that point. I believed at the time that there was no baby until twelve weeks following conception. I also did not know that there was anything wrong with having an abortion. I was sure that having an abortion was no different than curing a disease.

I had only a limited worldly point of reference at the time.

Promises to Keep

Fear of man will prove to be a snare, but whoever trusts in the Lord is kept safe.
Proverbs 29:25

I was living in a world that declared new freedoms: freedom to love one another without fear of pregnancy, freedom to control when one would have children, and freedom from sexually transmitted diseases (STDs), as most known or recognized STDs could then be cured. It was the time of the sexual revolution. It was also the time for a new awakening in the movement for women's liberation and equality. Women were now free to pursue careers and expect equal pay for equal work. It was no longer lawful to discriminate against women in employment. There was freedom for women to have it all. The freedom to have an abortion was part of that world. It had been legalized by our Supreme Court just two years earlier.

I know now that I was wrong. I didn't know it then. I was misguided and misinformed. All I knew was that I needed to keep it a secret. I couldn't let anyone know. At first I kept the secret so that no one would ever know that I had gotten pregnant. Later, however, as I heard conversations between friends and family members, I began to realize that not everyone perceived abortion as an acceptable choice. I watched news reports about picketing, rioting, bombing and even killing at abortion clinics. I observed the look of disgust in the eyes of a medical worker when I admitted to choosing abortion. I saw in my pregnancy books while I was pregnant with our first daughter the pictures of a growing fetus, week after week. It was a baby right from the start.

In time, I began to question the acceptability of my choice. Was I guilty of killing my baby? I'd wonder.

I recall taking our daughters to the children's museum. In the health section, I could not help but pause with sadness as I viewed the picture depicting the baby inside the mother's womb at ten weeks old. I could not help but wonder about my lost baby. Then I'd feel my guilt. I couldn't change the past, so I'd drive the feelings of guilt deeply into my core, hoping they would never surface again.

Time and time again, though, with every reminder of the aborted baby, the feelings of guilt would surface. I tried to deny that I was guilty. It's over. It was long ago. There is nothing that you can do about it. Forget it, I'd tell myself. Then, as though I couldn't stop my thoughts, I'd think again about the lost baby. What would he be like now? I'd wonder.

> **Promises to Keep**
>
> Sons are a heritage from the Lord, children a reward from him.
>
> Psalm 127:3

Ultimately, my secret was not being kept to hide the fact that I had gotten pregnant, but rather to hide the fact that I had chosen abortion. In my heart, I was guilty of making an unacceptable choice. It was unacceptable even though it was legal. And I couldn't fix it. I couldn't tell the baby that I was sorry. I couldn't bring the baby back to life. I was guilty of my choice. I chose a death sentence for my baby. Who could do such a thing? I'd ask in my heart. My answers, maybe they were Satan's answers, created shame.

When my grandmother died, I wondered if she would meet my baby in heaven. When I thought about my grandmother, heaven and the afterlife, the everlasting impact of the abortion hit me. Although the actual procedure for the abortion lasted only a short time, I suddenly and fearfully understood that the impact would last a lifetime. No, not a lifetime, the impact would last forever, into eternity.

I could no longer deny the truth about abortion. I could only continue to bury my feelings deep within my heart. Ignore it. There is nothing that can be done.

I tried running from the shame, trying to hide it from others through success. Do your best and be successful, show kindness to others, and prove to everyone that you are a good person. Prove it, prove it, and prove it again.

My shame began to surface through my efforts to be the person that I thought everyone believed that I should be. I craved positive feedback. I craved acceptance by all. Show them that you are a worthy person through your hard work and appropriate behavior. Work harder, stick to the rules, show respect, be the perfect mother, and do what is right at all times. Give no one any reason to find fault with you. My shame led to a personal standard that was impossible to maintain. In new situations, I would try to read from others' comments and their body language what characteristics would be acceptable to them. I'd then try to portray those characteristics. I lost my true identity by trying to hide my shame.

As I worked harder and harder to be the person that I thought I should be, Satan seemed to spin the world faster and faster and faster. I once described my world as moving so fast that I was afraid that I could no longer hang on. I drew a picture of it. There was the round ball called Earth. On it was a lone, leafless tree sticking straight up; and on the branches of that tree I grasped for my life to keep from falling away from the world. As the earth turned faster and faster, my body was carried by the centrifugal force to a position perpendicular to the earth's surface as I clung to the branches of the tree. The tree was the only thing keeping me from being flung away from the earth, into darkness. My feet were no longer grounded by gravity. My only hope for survival, I believed, was through my own strength, and I was getting tired.

Satan was hoping that I'd lose my grip. Fortunately for me, the tree became the cross of Christ, and I didn't need to rely on my strength alone.

When I was 38 years old, I found Jesus Christ. I thought that I knew him before, but I only knew of him. I finally asked him to be my Savior, to forgive my sins and to be in my life. He came to me that day through the Holy Spirit. I finally accepted him, and began to know what it meant to have a relationship with him.

As part of my newly found relationship with Christ, I knew that Christ died for my sins and that I was forgiven. However, I still held tightly to the shame. The shame was part of me, but I had taken the first steps on the right path.

Healing deep scars can take a very long time; but God has healed my wounds. While I don't believe that I can make direct restitution for my choice to have an abortion, God provided the forgiveness that I sought. Although I can never during my lifetime on Earth be reconciled with my unborn baby, God showed me signs of reconciliation with him and through my other children. I have found the way to peace: I walk in God's light, following him, listening for him, and seeking him.

The shame is gone.

> **Promises to Keep**
>
> I sought the Lord, and he answered me; he delivered me from all my fears. Those who look to him are radiant; their faces are never covered with shame.
>
> Psalm 34:4-5

Your Story

Shame is Everywhere

we're not alone

You may not share in my story of abortion. However, you may have your own personal source of shame. Shame is everywhere!

Shame comes from a myriad of sources; and because it manifests itself in a variety of ways, statistically defining the prevalence of shame is very hard. Most studies concern the ultimate problem for which shame might be either the result or an underlying cause. For example, deep-seated feelings of shame may result from child abuse and neglect. The studies, however, focus on the number of people that were victims of child abuse rather than the percentage of those people that faced diagnosable symptoms of shame as a result of the abuse.

For 2010, the U.S. Department of Health and Human Services (2006) reported that about 868,000 children were victims of childhood maltreatment.[1] The percentage of those children that will develop a sense of shame to the degree that it manifests itself as a behavior requiring some form of intervention is not known. However, one study found that about 80% of young adults that were abused as children met the diagnostic criteria for at least one psychological disorder.[2]

According to the Rape, Abuse, & Incest National Network, there are about 208,000 victims of sexual assualt reported in the United States each year, and it is estimated that more than half of all sexual assaults go unreported.[3] Victims of rape, sexual abuse or incest are three times more likely to suffer from depression, six times more likely to suffer from post-traumatic stress disorder, thirteen times more likely to abuse alcohol, and twenty-six times more likely to abuse drugs.[4] While all of these are ways in which shame symptoms might manifest themselves, it is unknown how many of these cases involve a serious or diagnosable level of shame felt by the victims.

Finally, in a study of about 5600 men and women, the Florida State University found that the people that said they were verbally abused by their parents (about 30% of those surveyed), had 1.6 times more symptoms of depression and anxiety than those that were not verbally abused. Children that are verbally abused by their parents ultimately believe the negative feedback and then develop a pattern of self-criticism. Such a person will regularly blame himself for any adverse or disappointing event.[5] Excessive self-criticism is one of the ways in which shame symptoms can be seen.

The above studies focus on external forces or actions which may have caused the victims to feel shame. Remember, however, that shame can also be self-imposed through unresolved guilt (perhaps for a criminal act, an accident causing harm to another, or for lawful, but regrettable actions such as choosing an abortion), or through circumstances that involve no actual fault or personal choice (perhaps through a corporate downsizing or extended unemployment or other events which causes serious or prolonged embarrassment), or simply because a person is prone to feel shame more readily than the average person. However, I am unaware of any statistical studies identifying the extent that shame may be tied to these types of events or issues.

According to Dr. Daniel Green and Mel Lawrenz, authors of Encountering Shame and Guilt, "guilt and shame are the central human problems; other problems are outgrowths of these issues."[6] Additionally, they note that "the Christian gospel has always said that the universal spiritual crisis in the human race is guilt and shame."[7] Based on these expert opinions, I think that it is safe to say guilt and shame affects the entire human race in some form. Some shame presents itself in a psychologically diagnosable manner. Some shame does not.

The genesis of shame is fear. Some of the shame that we feel is healthy, because God will use our fears to guide us away from things that may make us feel guilt or shame. Satan will use our fears to trap us in guilt and shame, making our shame debilitating. In those instances, people often develop a web of lies within which they live, often unbeknownst to even themselves, and often harmful not only to themselves but also to others.[8]

Satan loves it when we get stuck in the wallowing depths of shame. It is through such shame that he will try to separate you from the love of God. Carrying the burden of shame, regardless of its source, is exhausting. It's like carrying all of our problems in a big saddlebag on our backs, like a pack mule. Wouldn't it be great to leave the saddlebag behind? When I shed my shame, it felt like a successful diet. I began to feel comfortable in my own skin. I felt new freedom to move forward in life with the love of Christ and renewed self-assurance. I now know peace.

I encourage you to question whether Satan is stealing your joy through shame. I pray that you will be able to identify the difference between shame to be shed and healthy shame with which to resolve, and the consequences of guilt with which to grapple. To determine the differences, it will be necessary to first understand the truth of the matter. Did you actually do something wrong or fail to do something? Is there anything that you might do to make restitution or to find reconciliation? Do you have a behavior that you would like to modify? If the answers to one or more of these questions are yes, start now to try to resolve the situation. If your shame was inappropriately imposed upon you by someone else, or accepted by you as the result of another's guilt, perhaps you are living with a shame that does not belong to you. Then, it is time to let go. Give it to our loving Father. Give it to Jesus. Let Christ carry the burden for you.

> **Promises to Keep**
>
> Come to me, all you who are weary and burdened, and I will give you rest. Take my yoke upon you and learn from me, for I am gentle and humble in heart, and you will find rest for your souls. For my yoke is easy and my burden is light.
>
> Jesus, Matthew 11:28-30

Notes

1. U.S. Department of Health and Human Services, Administration on Children, Youth and Families, Children's Bureau. (2011) *Child Maltreatment 2010.*

2. Child Welfare Information Gateway. "Long Term Consequences of Child Abuse and Neglect." April 2006. U.S. Department of Health and Human Services. November 07, 2006 <http://www.childwelfare.gov/pubs/factsheets/long_term_conssequences.cfm>.

3. Rape, Abuse & Incest National Network. "Statistics." 2013. May 27, 2013 <http://www.rainn.org/statistics>.

4. Rape, Abuse & Incest National Network. "Effects of Rape." 2006, June 12, 2006 <http://www.rainn.org/statistics/effects-of-rape.html>.

5. Elish, Jill. "Verbal Abuse in Childhood Triggers Adult Anxiety, Depression." May 24, 2006. Medical News Today. June 19, 2006 <http://www.medicalnewstoday.com/medicalnews.php ?newsid=43894>.

6. Green, Daniel and Mel Lawrenz. *Encountering Shame and Guilt.* Grand Rapids, MI: Baker Books, a division of Baker Book House Company, 1994 by Daniel R. Green and Mel Lawrenz. Page 127.

7. Green, Daniel and Mel Lawrenz. *Encountering Shame and Guilt.* Grand Rapids, MI: Baker Books, a division of Baker Book House Company, 1994 by Daniel R. Green and Mel Lawrenz. Page 28.

8. For more on the web of lies people create and their genesis in fear, see Peck, M. Scott, M.D. *People of the Lie: The Hope for Healing Human Evil.* New York, NY: Touchstone, 1983 by M. Scott Peck, M.D.

I'm Exhausted!

Week 1

shame is a heavy burden

*The Lord is close to the brokenhearted
and saves those who are crushed in spirit.*

Psalm 34:18

Welcome & Purpose

Welcome to the Grapple with Guilt, Shed the Shame covenant support group intended for all men and women who may be struggling with unresolved guilt or feelings of shame, regardless of the source.

The purpose of the group is:

to share the love, grace, and mercy of Christ Jesus with each other by sharing and bearing each other's burdens, expressing our love and care for one another, and encouraging each other so that we might find healing, hope, and joy.

Opening Prayer

Dear God, our Father in heaven. We thank you for your loving and merciful presence with us this day. You know that we often carry feelings of regret, doubt, fear, shame, and unworthiness. Sometimes, we don't fully understand the source of these feelings or the extent to which they are impacting our lives. Frequently, we don't know how to find relief from the burdens that these feelings create. As we meet in this covenant group, studying your Word, we ask that you bless us with your presence. Open our eyes to the underlying matters that have impacted us in unhealthy ways. Bless us with understanding and heal our hearts. Struggling with guilt and shame makes us weary, but we know that you will give us strength, through your son, Jesus Christ. Amen.

Meeting & Greeting

Each of us might be feeling a little uncomfortable or even nervous. But I'm certain that those feelings will subside once we get to know each other better.

❶ Please introduce yourselves. Tell us your name and something positive and special about yourself.

_____

_____

_____

_____

_____

Our Group Covenant

This group is a covenant group. Covenants help us to build trust, share openly, and love and care for each other on the hills and in the valleys of our lives. A covenant group is based in love, and ultimately a promise to treat everyone in the group with love. You know what love is.

"Love is patient, love is kind. It does not envy, it does not boast, it is not proud. It is not rude, it is not self-seeking, it is not easily angered, and it keeps no record of wrongs. Love does not delight in evil but rejoices with the truth. It always protects, always trusts, always hopes, always perseveres." (1 Corinthians 13:4-8)

Some people are very comfortable sharing their thoughts, feelings, concerns, worries, or fears within a group context. Somehow they live with a sense of love, trust, and freedom. But for many of us, it takes a while to build that feeling of confidence and trust with the others in the group. For some of us, someone in our past broke the trust we gave to them, causing deep hurts.

Trust is needed before true sharing is possible. Trust is based on the knowledge that all group participants will respect one another, will be honest, will keep confidences, and will not gossip or criticize. Trust is based on the knowledge that all group participants will treat each other with love.

Developing this trust can take months or even years of friendship within typical life circumstances. However, we need this sense of trust to begin building today, in order for our group to make the most of each weekly session.

To help resolve this issue, it is important to obtain everyone's promise to be loving, trustworthy friends, brothers, and sisters in Christ.

Getting Started

When you signed up for this group, you were each provided with this Grapple with Guilt, Shed the Shame workbook. As homework for this first session, you may have been asked to read the introductory materials, including the sections entitled "Using This Workbook," "Guilt and Shame: what are these?," "Now I Live in Peace! the author's story," and "Shame is Everywhere." If you did not read these things, please commit to do so before the next session.

These materials will help you understand the concepts of guilt and shame as used in this workbook. You will also learn about the author's experience with unresolved guilt and the resultant shame. While you may not share in her circumstances, reading about her feelings of shame, and the heavy burden caused by shame-based living, you may begin to recognize areas of unresolved guilt or shame in your own life.

❷ Describe the affects of the shame felt by the author in her story?

_____

_____

_____

_____

I'm Exhausted! Shame is a Heavy Burden

This section provides examples of how carrying the burden of shame can be an exhausting endeavor, regardless of its source. We ultimately require extra strength or courage to take the steps needed to grow beyond the shame. Through these stories, you will discover a variety of ways that a person dealing with unresolved guilt or with shame will feel. Volunteers are encouraged to read this piece aloud.

Joel's Story

We lived in a small town, where the majority of the residents were either Catholic or Lutheran. Of course, then, most of my friends were either Catholic or Lutheran. For whatever reason, my parents stopped going to church when I was young. So I wasn't baptized either as a baby like my friends had been, or later as a child. Because our church involvement was so limited, I didn't fully understand my friends when they referred to First Communion, Confirmation or Catechism class. As time went on, whenever friends talked about their church experiences, I felt embarrassed for not being like them. However, I didn't really know what I should do about that embarrassment. I just wanted to keep my lack of church experiences a secret. I especially didn't want to explain to anyone that I had not been baptized. Sometimes I lied about it to avoid the need to explain. I was afraid of being different, labeled and left out. I just wanted to blend with the crowd, and not have this point become a reason to stand out. As an adult, I chose to be baptized in a private ceremony, still embarrassed about having waited so long. Even today, in some circles, it is assumed that I would have been baptized as an infant or in my youth. I sometimes feel guilty for having waited so long.
— Joel

Jackie's Story

I couldn't believe that she lied to me! It put me in an awful position. I knew I should have double checked her work; but I had been recently chastised by my boss for not trusting my employees and relying on their experience. Apparently, she had complained to him that I kept too close of tabs on her in spite of her extensive experience. So, for the first time I did not insist on seeing her file. She promised that she had everything documented and placed in the file; but, in reality, she had kept almost no records. The file was critical to the decision that was made. I was going to be blamed! I felt so awful. I thought that I'd lose my job once my boss learned what happened. I couldn't sleep, just thinking about it. I felt so guilty about not doing my job the way that I believed was best. There was ultimately a lawsuit and it took a couple years for the situation to be resolved, all the while I felt at fault even though I had followed my boss's instructions. When I prayed about my fears and guilt, I asked God for an answer, for help, for reassurances. I opened my Bible and began reading. God must have directed my fingers to this particular page. I began reading about Christ's crucifixion. Oh no! I thought to myself. I'm going to be crucified at work! I was so distraught, I totally missed the point. — Jackie

> **Promises to Keep**
>
> The Lord your God is with you
> he is mighty to save.
> He will take great delight in you,
> he will quiet you with his love,
> he will rejoice over you with singing.
> 									Zephaniah 3:17

Sandy's Story

I hid it for years. Even my best friends didn't know. I couldn't let them know that I had a baby when I was just eighteen, and that I gave him to another family through adoption. I was afraid of their reaction. What would they think of me? I was ashamed of the fact that I had sex with my boyfriend, without regard to the potential consequences. Did I really think that I wouldn't get pregnant? How could I have been so careless? I knew better. My boyfriend and I had actually broken up; but then we got back together for that brief time. I knew I didn't love him. I was sent away at the time to hide the fact that I was pregnant from the people in the community. Being pregnant and not married was considered shameful in that community, at that time. I was sure that everyone knew, though. I hated that town and everything that it represented. I felt shameful. Why did I ever allow it to happen? I wasn't ashamed of the baby. I was ashamed of me. The shame was a heavy burden. The anger still lingers, even though it has been years. —Sandy

> **Promises to Keep**
>
> He has sent me to bind up the brokenhearted,
> …to bestow on them a crown of beauty instead of ashes, the oil of gladness instead of mourning, and a garment of praise instead of a spirit of despair.
> 									Isaiah 61:1,3

Whatever our source of guilt, whatever our shame, we often find a need to try to hide the issue from our friends, our families, and our community. Some of us carry our secrets for years. Sometimes we hide simply by being quiet. Sometimes we hide by trying to be the person that we believe all others expect us to be. Sometimes we hide by trying to be all things to all people, as the author did to hide her choice of having chosen abortion, creating an impossible burden to carry. The secret, the shame, the burden will eventually wear one down. It will eventually exhaust you. If the burden is not resolved, your world might soon seem like it is spinning out of control, just as in the author's story as she tried to hide from her past by being all things to everyone. Strength is needed to hold on as the world seems to spin out of control.

We need to slow down, calm down, and seek God's help for our tormented souls. Then, accept his love. Don't miss the point.

> **Promises to Keep**
>
> God is my refuge and strength,
> an ever-present help in trouble.
> Psalm 46:1

Do I Suffer from Shame?

Some things we can just forget, other things press upon our hearts for many years. Sometimes it is simple embarrassment, other times we feel we can do or take no more. Some of us are shame-prone, meaning that we feel shame over the smallest of infractions or perceived infractions. Others seem to feel no pain, no shame whatsoever, regardless of what they have done.

❸ Not all shame is felt to the same degree. Compare the degrees of guilt and/or shame described in the above stories and in the author's introductory story.

_____

_____

_____

_____

❹ Describe the various ways guilt and shame might impact a person.

❺ As a group, share additional stories where you or someone that you know felt the impact of guilt or shame. (Please do not share names.) Discuss how the guilt or shame may have impacted the person's personality or relationships with others, or the person's sense of satisfaction with his or her life circumstances.

❻ In the author's personal story, she tried to be all things to all people, and this eventually overwhelmed her. Discuss why carrying shame or hiding one's past from others might become exhausting?

❼ Share ideas on what a person might do to relieve this feeling of exhaustion.

_____

_____

_____

_____

_____

❽ Take a few minutes to review the following checklist quietly to yourselves. Pick a few of the questions and discuss how the issue described might be the result of shame.

_____

_____

_____

_____

—Would you describe yourself as a workaholic?
—Have you been told that you are too demanding at work?
—Do you get inordinately defensive when receiving constructive criticism?
—Do you feel better about yourself when you are around others that are less qualified or less skilled than you?
—Do you frequently compare yourself with others, finding fault in yourself as a result?
—Were your parents dissatisfied with you and your choices in life?
—Were your parents physically or emotionally abusive to you?
—Do you feel better about yourself when you criticize others?
—Were you bullied or harassed as a child?
—Do you feel that you are a square peg in a round hole when you are in social or work settings?
—Are you exceptionally shy?
—Do you question whether most other people in your work or social circles really like you?

—Do you frequently say that you are sorry, even when you have no part in or control of the situation, accepting undeserved blame?
—Pick five words to describe yourself. Are these primarily negative words?
—When you look in the mirror each day, are you frequently dissatisfied with the reflection?
—Do you try to do everything perfectly out of fear of an adverse reaction from others?
—Do you avoid socializing with other people?
—Do you avoid conversations that may involve heartfelt sharing of thoughts and feelings?
—Do you find it hard to look others in the eye when talking?
—Do you tend to dwell on your mistakes?
—Do you have difficulty forgiving yourself when you make a mistake?
—Do you have feelings of inadequacy that seem to never go away?
—Are you emotionally numb, unable to allow your feelings of love or attachment toward others to grow?
—Are you so afraid of failure that you avoid doing new things?
—Are you an alcoholic or drug abuser?
—Are you a "super-pleaser", seeking to gain approval from all those around you?
—Do you have unrelenting feelings of sadness or bouts with depression?
—Do you have feelings of suicide?
—Do you often feel like an outsider, even among friends or people that you know?
—Do you repeatedly ask God to forgive you for a past action or inaction as though it is an unforgivable sin?
—Are you afraid that if you let your guard down, others will discover who you really are?
—Do you have trouble accepting or believing positive feedback?
—Do you crave positive feedback?
—Do you feel like you can never do the job or task well enough?
—Do you often belittle yourself?
—Are you critical of the things that you do or say, expecting perfection?

— Do you often minimize your feelings of hurt, anger or disappointment?
— Do you try to always present yourself to others as being strong and independent, regardless of how you really feel?
— Do you believe that you are a failure in one or more of your life's roles (parent, child, employee, Christian or friend)?

9 Read the following list of questions and discuss why feelings like these might be considered good or healthy?

- Do you get embarrassed if you mistakenly break or differ from the social norm?

- Do you recognize your personal imperfections, and work to improve yourself? At the same time, are you able to accept those personal imperfections that cannot be changed?

- Have you developed a personal set of values and morals to which you try to live? Do you recognize with remorse when you breach any of your values or morals?

- Does your sense of humility enable you to appreciate with love the people around you?

- Does your sense of humility encourage you to find strength through a relationship with God?

10 Fear causes many of us to make choices that lead to guilt or shame. Please share an example of when fear caused you or someone you know to do something that that person knew was wrong.

_____

_____

_____

_____

Bible Study

Please have one or more volunteers read the following stories from Luke 8:41-56.

Then a man named Jairus, a ruler of the synagogue, came and fell at Jesus' feet, pleading with him to come to his house because his only daughter, a girl of about twelve, was dying.

As Jesus was on his way, the crowds almost crushed him. And a woman was there who had been subject to bleeding for twelve years, but no one could heal her. She came up behind him and touched the edge of his cloak, and immediately her bleeding stopped.

"Who touched me?" Jesus asked.

When they all denied it, Peter said, "Master, the people are crowding and pressing against you."

But Jesus said, "Someone touched me; I know that power has gone out from me."

Then the woman, seeing that she could not go unnoticed, came trembling and fell at his feet. In the presence of all the people, she told why she had touched him and how she had been instantly healed. Then he said to her, "Daughter, your faith has healed you. Go in peace."

While Jesus was still speaking, someone came from the house of Jairus, the synagogue ruler. "Your daughter is dead," he said, "Don't bother the teacher any more."

Hearing this, Jesus said to Jairus, "Don't be afraid; just believe, and she will be healed."

When he arrived at the house of Jairus, he did not let anyone go in with him except Peter, John and James, and the child's father and mother. Meanwhile, all the people were wailing and mourning for her. "Stop wailing," Jesus said. "She is not dead but asleep."

They laughed at him, knowing that she was dead. But he took her by the hand and said, "My child, get up!" Her spirit returned, and at once she stood up. Then Jesus told them to give her something to eat. Her parents were astonished, but he ordered them not to tell anyone what had happened.

11 The woman that touched Jesus' cloak had been bleeding for 12 years, and no one could heal her. Similarly, some people carry their feelings of shame for many years. Discuss why people might carry shame for many years, finding no relief or healing for their hearts.

_____

_____

12 Jesus told the woman that her faith healed her. What did she do to exhibit her faith?

13 What does this passage suggest that we might do to shed our feelings of shame?

14 Jairus was told not to bother Jesus because his daughter was already dead. But, what did Jesus tell him?

15 When we carry feelings of shame for many years, we often begin to believe that there is nothing that can possibly help. What do we learn from the story of Jairus about Jesus' ability to heal?

_____

_____

_____

_____

Please read aloud the following verses from Isaiah 40:28b-31.

The Lord is the everlasting God,
the Creator of the ends of the earth.
He will not grow tired or weary,
and his understanding no one can fathom.
He gives strength to the weary
and increases the power of the weak.
Even youths grow tired and weary,
and young men stumble and fall;
But those who hope in the Lord
will renew their strength.
They will soar on wings like eagles;
they will run and not grow weary,
they will walk and not be faint.

16 Based on the above passage from Isaiah, describe in your own words the kind of strength that God can give to us when we are in need of help?

_____

_____

_____

_____

_____

Reflection & Encouragement

"Life is not a level, smooth path, but rather a series of hills and valleys. There are times spent on the mountain top, when everything seems clear and perfect. Then there are those times when we feel like we're wandering around in a dark cavern. Take a moment and set your heart to be persistent in your faith - faith in God to lead you, pick you up when you have fallen, give you strength to go on, and ultimately bring you to victory."

—from *Coffee Break with God*

Closing Prayer

Father, God, the creator of all of the heavens and the earth. Your strength has no limits. In contrast, we know that our strength is limited. Sometimes we tire ourselves with our burdens of shame, and we need your strength to move forward in our faith and in our love for you and for one another. Thank you for providing the strength that we need and for carrying us when we are weak. In time, help us to understand the source of our weariness, and enable us to overcome it through faith in you and the saving power of your son, Jesus Christ. In his name we pray. Amen.

Week 1 Memory Verse

For the eyes of the Lord range throughout the earth to strengthen those whose hearts are fully committed to him.

2 Chronicles 16:9

Homework

1. Return to the checklist under question 8 and determine which, if any, questions describe you. If you have checked a number of questions as describing yourself, you may be suffering from some form of shame to an unhealthy degree.

2. Ask God through prayer to reveal to you possible situations of unresolved guilt or experiences causing shame. In your prayer, seek first his timing for revealing these situations, and then his strength and wisdom regarding them.

3. Start a journal, with the first entry being a list of shaming circumstances in your life. A journal is simply a place where you write down your thoughts as directed in this study as well as other thoughts that come to mind. It can be a spiral notebook or a journaling book that you purchased. It is easy to write, because you are writing it for your eyes only. There is

no need to worry about complete sentences, spelling, or grammar. The purpose is to help you think about what is on your mind and to verbalize those thoughts for your own review and consideration.

❹ Pray over this list as written in your journal, asking God to broaden your understanding regarding each item listed so that you are able to put the situation in context and to begin to understand God's truth concerning each situation.

❺ Please read Week 2 in preparation for the next meeting.

Why Would God Help Me?

Week 2

I'm so unworthy

> [Because] you are precious and honored in my sight, and because I love you.
>
> Isaiah 43:4

Opening Prayer

Dear Holy Father, over the years many of us have learned that we do not stand up to the standards set for us, standards set either by others or by ourselves. We also know that we have sinned in many ways. As sinners, we have failed our friends, our families, ourselves and you, perhaps by things we have done or perhaps by things that we didn't do. In spite of our failures, we are able to come to you through your never ending grace, seeking your love. Thank you, dear Father for your love and your mercy. Help us, today, to grow in understanding of your love for us. In Jesus' name we pray. Amen.

Meeting & Greeting

Welcome to our second week in this Grapple with Guilt, Shed the Shame covenant group. To open the conversation, let's go around the room and introduce ourselves again.

❶ This week, tell us about something you remember praying for as a child. Maybe you prayed for a new bicycle or a pony, or maybe you prayed for a new baby brother or sister.

_____

_____

48 / Grapple with Guilt

_____

_____

_____

Getting Started

2 If you are willing, please share a story of when you or a friend felt humiliation over an embarrassing moment, humiliation to a degree that you or your friend just wanted to go home and avoid having to face anyone.

_____

_____

_____

_____

_____

3 Discuss as a group, how embarrassing moments might make us feel shame?

_____

_____

_____

_____

_____

Why Would God Help Me? I'm So Unworthy

This section provides examples of how shame can make us believe that we are unworthy of love. Through these stories, you will discover a variety of ways that a person dealing with unresolved guilt or with shame might believe that he or she is unlovable. Volunteers are encouraged to read this piece aloud.

Anna's Story

When I was a child, my mother made me feel ashamed that I existed. Her favorite line, or at least the line that I remember being the clearest, was "I never wanted any of you kids. If I had my way, none of you would ever have been born." I felt guilty for even existing. I always wondered what I was doing wrong. Why was I such a burden? I'd wonder. I spent most of my childhood trying to be as passive and inconspicuous as possible so that my mother would not leave us with just our father. (He had his own set of problems.)

We, as children, were never touched or told, "I love you." If you needed a hug or any reassurance, you were deemed to be too needy…which was looked upon as being something terrible. Whenever I told my mother that I was invited to do something with a friend's family, her first response was always something like, "Why would they want you to go along? They probably don't really want you along but are just trying to be nice."

My fondest memories of childhood were those that I created in my mind involving my self-made, imaginary family. In my imaginary family, I was one of six siblings. I was the youngest of them by many years, and everyone doted on me. How embarrassing to think that my happiest memories from childhood only existed in my mind. Not only did I feel shame for simply living, but I felt shame for creating and living with my imaginary family.

Ultimately, I learned not to trust anyone, and the only one I knew that I could rely upon was me. It was almost impossible for me to be happy. By twelve years of age, I would lie in my bed at night and pray to God that he would just let me die. I'd plead with him, "I've had enough of this life and if this is how my life is going to be, please don't put me through the torture. Take me now!" Of course, God didn't take me. He doesn't want me either, I concluded to myself.

Promises to Keep

Why then did you bring me out of the womb? I wish I had died before any eye saw me. If only I had never come into being, or had been carried straight from the womb to the grave!

                                                Job, Job 10:18-19

I have to say, though, the greatest shame I feel today comes from being very close to giving up my life by my own hands. I have spent at least five years, even more, trying to get over my feelings of shame and realizing that it was not my fault. It's like I was spitting in God's face when I was so upset because he wouldn't let me die. I thought I knew better than God. If he won't kill me, then I will. —Anna

> **Promises to Keep**
>
> But God does not take away life; instead, he devises ways so that a banished person may not remain estranged from him.
>
> 2 Samuel 14:14

There are many things that happen to us that make us feel unlovable, unqualified, not valuable, or unworthy. Many people, just like Anna, were repeatedly told by their parents that they were not loved and that they were something less than a child. Some people will recall that they could never live up to their parents' unrealistic expectations.

But we are not worthless. God loves each of us deeply. He has plans for our lives.

> **Promises to Keep**
>
> "For I know the plans I have for you," declares the LORD, "plans to prosper you and not to harm you, plans to give you hope and a future."
>
> Jeremiah 29:11

❹ Why did Anna feel shameful?

_____

_____

_____

_____

_____

❺ We can simply assume that no child would deserve the comments and verbal abuse that Anna received.

Discuss what personal or internal issues a parent might be struggling with which would cause that parent to say such things to his or her child.

_____

_____

_____

_____

_____

6 When God did not take Anna's life, as she hoped in her prayers, Anna concluded that even God didn't want her. List at least five possible reasons as to why Anna's conclusion was not correct.

_____

_____

_____

_____

_____

> **Promises to Keep**
> And so we know and rely on the love God has for us. God is love.
> 1 John 4:16

Bible Study

Because Anna prayed to God for help, it is apparent that she knew of him and believed in him. However, when he did not answer her prayer in the manner that she had hoped, she concluded that he did not want her or love her. Please ask a volunteer to read Genesis 1, verses 26 and 27, as printed below.

Then God said, "Let us make man in our image, in our likeness, and let them rule over the fish of the sea and the birds of the air, over the livestock, over all the earth, and over all the creatures that move along the ground.
So God created man in his own image,
in the image of God he created him;

male and female he created them.

7 What does it mean to be in the image of God? (If you have a dictionary, look up the meaning of the word, image.)

_____
_____
_____
_____
_____

8 List at least 5 possible reasons why God might have made man in his own image?

_____
_____
_____
_____
_____

9 It is common to see someone's child and then make a comment on whether the child resembles the mother or the father. Typically, what do you think a parent feels when a friend says that a child is his or her "spitting image?"

_____
_____
_____
_____
_____

Again, please read verses 15 - 17 from Romans, Ch. 8.

For you did not receive a spirit that makes you a slave again to fear, but you received the Spirit of sonship. And by him we cry, "Abba, Father." The Spirit himself testifies with our spirit that we are God's children. Now if we are children, then we are heirs - heirs of God and co-heirs with Christ, if indeed we share in his sufferings in order that we may also share in his glory.

❿ It is clear from these passages that God has made us his children, co-heirs with Christ, and that we can call God our father. Describe how God as our heavenly father might be similar to our earthly parents.

_____

_____

_____

_____

_____

⓫ Describe also how God as our heavenly father might be different than our earthly parents.

_____

_____

_____

_____

_____

Let us now read more specifically about God's love for us.

How great is the love the Father has lavished on us, that we should be called children of God! And that is what we are!

1 John 3:1

Whoever does not love does not know God, because God is love. This is how God showed his love among us: He sent his one and only Son into the world that we might live through him. This is love: not that we loved God, but that he loved us and sent his Son as an atoning sacrifice for our sins.

1 John 4:8-10

For I am convinced that neither death nor life, neither angels nor demons, neither the present nor the future, nor any powers, neither height nor depth, nor anything else in all creation, will be able to separate us from the love of God that is in Christ Jesus our Lord.

Romans 8:38-39

12 How has God shown us that he loves us?

_____

_____

_____

_____

_____

13 What, if anything in particular, must we do to become worthy of God's love? See 1 John 4:8-10 as printed above.

_____

_____

_____

_____

_____

14 Anna believed that she may have done something wrong to make her mother dislike her. She also believed that God did not like her. Do you agree with Anna? Why or why not? (Consider the verses quoted from Romans 8 when answering this question.)

_____

_____

_____

_____

Anna appears to have believed that God did not answer her prayers. To know his answer to her prayers, read Psalm 91:14-16 as printed below.

> "Because he loves me," says the Lord, "I will rescue him;
> I will protect him, for he acknowledges my name.
> He will call upon me, and I will answer him;
> I will be with him in trouble,
> I will deliver him and honor him.

*With long life will I satisfy him
and show him my salvation."*

⑮ God did not grant Anna her request to die. Based on the passage above, list at least 5 things that God may have done for Anna instead.

_____

_____

_____

_____

_____

Reflection & Encouragement

"Oneword frees us of all theweight and pain of life: That word is love."

Sophocles

"No father or mother has loved you as God has, for it was that you might be happy He gave His only Son. When He bowed His head in the death hour, love solemnized its triumph; the sacrifice there was complete."

Henry Wadsworth Longfellow

Closing Prayer

Let's close with a prayer that has been adapted in part from the prayer that the Apostle Paul prayed for the people of Ephesus and for all believers in Jesus Christ. (See Ephesians 3:14-21.)

Today, we kneel before you, our Father, from whom your whole family in heaven and on earth derives its name. We pray that out of your glorious riches you may strengthen each of us with power through your Spirit in our inner beings, so that Christ may dwell in our hearts though faith. And we pray that we, being rooted and established in love, may have power, together with all the saints, to grasp how wide and long and high and deep is the love of Christ, and to know this love that surpasses knowledge - that we may be filled to the measure of all the fullness of you, O God. Now to you, dear Father, being able to do immeasurably more than all we ask or imagine, according to your power that is at work within us, to you be glory in the church and in

Christ Jesus throughout all generations, for ever and ever! We thank you. We praise you. All honor and glory are yours. Amen.

Week 2 Memory Verse

Yet to all who received him, to those who believed in his name, he gave the right to become children of God.

John 1:12

Homework

① In your journal, make a list of ways that God has blessed you. The list might include special people in your life, ways that he has protected you in times of trouble, things that have given you comfort over the years, and signs of his forgiveness or other signs of his love. Make the list as long as you can. I challenge you to come up with at least 25 items.

② Pray over this list, thanking God for his never-ending love as seen through these blessings.

③ God answers our prayers, sometimes quickly, sometimes seemingly slowly, but always right on time in accordance with his plan. Sometimes his answers do not match our requests. In your journal, if you have any specific prayer requests throughout the weeks spent in this Bible study, note them and the dates of the requests. Leave room on the page to write God's answer. Come back to your journal when the prayer is answered, whether directly as requested or differently, or by simply letting the need disappear, and note the answer in your journal, along with the date.

④ Pray over the answered prayers with thanksgiving, especially when God's answer differs from your request. He knows the big picture, and he will answer according to his plan.

⑤ Please read Week 3 in preparation for the next meeting.

Week 3

If Only I Had . . .

our doubts and insecurities

> *So I find this law at work: When I want to do good, evil is right there with me.... What a wretched man I am! Who will rescue me from this body of death? Thanks be to God - through Jesus Christ our Lord!*
>
> Romans 7:21, 24-25 Isaiah 43:4

Opening Prayer

Dear Lord, God our Father. We know in our minds that you love us and that you call us your children. However, sometimes we feel so far away from you. This is especially true when we discover that we have not been the kind of person that you want us to be. Try as we might to do what is right and righteous, we continue to make mistakes. Help us, Lord, to draw near to you and to be more like your son, Jesus Christ in all that we think and do, and in all that we choose not to do. Help us to live out our love for you. Help us to draw near to you. In Jesus' name we pray. Amen.

Meeting & Greeting

Welcome to our third week in the Grapple with Guilt, Shed the Shame covenant group. Again, let's begin with introductions. Please tell us a little more about yourselves.

❶ This week, describe a time that you tried to help a friend or family member, but it just didn't turn out the way that you intended.

_____

_____

Getting Started

❷ Thinking about your homework regarding God's blessings, did anyone list something as a blessing that might seem unusual or unique to the group? Would you care to share it with the group?

___

❸ It is easy to see God's love through his blessings for us. Discuss your ideas on how we can see God's love when his blessings are not apparent (perhaps through times of trouble).

___

If Only I Had... Our Doubts & Insecurities

This section provides examples of how shame might enter into our lives through our doubts or insecurities. Through these stories, you will see how the "maybe I should have..." can begin to haunt us. Volunteers are encouraged to read this piece aloud.

Amber's Story

I'll never forget the time that I was babysitting a friend's toddler at my home. While watching him, an important long distance phone call came in on our land line. We didn't use a cell phone for our home-based calls at that time. Since I needed to take the call, another child that was in first grade took my friend's toddler upstairs to play. I was within ear shot of all of the kids in my charge, and I believed that everyone would be safe. When the toddler's mother came home, she made it clear to me that she did not appreciate that the kids were upstairs while I was on the phone. I apologized to her a number of times, but she didn't seem to accept my apology. Since then, I have always felt an uncomfortable edge as to her level of trust in me. Maybe I should not have taken that call. —Amber

Roger's Story

I hate going to hospitals or to nursing homes to visit a friend or relative. I don't know why I feel this way. It seems like I'm afraid to face their difficult situations. When my aunt was living in the nursing home and her mind and health were failing her, I couldn't get myself to visit her. *What do I say? I heard that she doesn't always make sense when she talks. What if I can't understand what she tries to say to me? What if she doesn't know me? Do we just sit together?* I'd fearfully ask myself many questions. So, letting my doubts and fears get the best of me, I'd come up with many excuses as to why I couldn't drive the thirty miles to visit. I'd silently argue with myself, *I should go visit her, but this is not a good time of day to visit. Besides, I have too much to do today. I could go tomorrow instead. But that won't work either. Maybe I'll go another day when my sister can go with me. Oh but she isn't going to be in town for weeks, and she can go only on weekends. I can't go on weekends.* Ultimately, I'd conclude, *Well, I'll think of something later.* Later never came. Then one week, I got a feeling or a sense that she was going to die that week. Maybe God was trying to tell me something. But again, the many excuses won all of my internal arguments. I concluded silently, *We are leaving for vacation in just a couple days. There is so much to get done before we can go. There is no way that I can take any time away before vacation. I can always visit her when we get back.* We left on our vacation, and while we were gone, she died. We couldn't get back in time for the funeral. I never showed her that I cared, even though I thought of her many times. How many years will this feeling last? I should have visited her when I had the chance. —Roger

> **Promises to Keep**
> As the scripture says, "Anyone who trusts in him will never be put to shame."
> Romans 10:11

Marian's Story

Our daughter was at a wedding shower near our home. It seemed like the perfect time to deliver to her that box of things from her room. That way she could take it to her place, sort it, and discard what she no longer wanted. It was going to be so much easier to meet her at this shower than to drive to her home, as she lived a couple hours away. Our stop would be just a minor interruption to the shower. Just as we arrived, the bride-to-be was just starting to open the gifts. When my daughter came outside, she just yelled at me, "Why did you have to bring this stuff here, right now? Couldn't you have waited?" She was clearly very angry. I couldn't understand how she could be so angry about such a small matter. Did she learn this behavior from me? I wondered. *Why does she always react so? Is it possible that I have reacted like this to her?* I felt shame for her, from her, and toward her, all the while wondering where I went wrong as I raised her. Should I have done something differently? —Marian

Alicia's Story

I got home from work at the usual time, and in my usual stressful way. There was always too much to do at work in the time allotted to get it done. As I hurried into the house, I noticed that our daughter, then a middle school student, wasn't home. Being gone at this time was unusual, so I asked our after-school nanny where she went. In reply, she paused and stammered a bit, finally saying, "Well she was upset and said that she needed a mom, so she went to her friend's house to see her friend's mom." "But she knows she can call me at work. I could have come home for her," I responded with impatience mixed with hurt feelings. Our nanny simply said, "She didn't think you'd want to be bothered." How devastated I was! I had always told my daughter that she could call me if she needed me. But, upon reflection, I knew that I had frequently answered her calls abruptly, told her to hurry to the point when calling me at work, or asked her if the call was truly important. I should have made my actions upon receiving her calls match my words encouraging her to call. If I had only handled her previous calls differently, maybe she wouldn't now look to another mom. —Alicia

The "should haves", "could haves", and "might haves" can really get to our hearts. We think about doing things right. We try to do our best. But, even with the best of intentions, we sometimes fail. Things don't always work out as intended. As the old saying goes, "We are only human." We may be only human, yet God still loves us.

> **Promises to Keep**
>
> As a father has compassion on his children, so the Lord has compassion on those who fear him; for he knows how we are formed, he remembers that we are dust.
>
> Psalm 103:13-14

❹ Please describe a time when you did something or failed to do something, and afterward you found yourself saying something like, "If only I had…," or "I should have…."

_____
_____
_____
_____
_____

❺ Describe how such regrets, doubts or questions might change a person's behavior in the future.

_____
_____
_____
_____
_____

6 Do you believe that it is healthy to have these regrets, doubts, or questions about our choices after it is too late to change the immediate situation? Why or why not? (Try to answer both sides of the issue.)

_____

_____

_____

_____

_____

Bible Study

Genesis is full of stories involving guilty actions, followed ultimately by shame. Please read the familiar account of Adam and Eve, from Genesis 2:21-25, Genesis 3:6-10 and Genesis 3:21-23.

So the Lord God caused the man to fall into a deep sleep; and while he was sleeping, he took one of the man's ribs and closed up the place with flesh. Then the Lord God made a woman from the rib he had taken out of the man, and he brought her to the man.
The man said,
"This is now bone of my bones
and flesh of my flesh;
she shall be called 'woman,'
for she was taken out of man."

For this reason a man will leave his father and mother and be united to his wife, and they will become one flesh. The man and his wife were both naked, and they felt no shame.

... When the woman saw that the fruit of the tree was good for food and pleasing to the eye, and also desirable for gaining wisdom, she took some and ate it. She also gave some to her husband, who was with her, and he ate it. Then the eyes of both of them were opened, and they realized they were naked; so they sewed fig leaves together and made coverings for themselves.

Then the man and his wife heard the sound of the Lord God as he was walking in the garden in the cool of the day, and they hid from the Lord God among the trees of the garden. But the Lord God called to the man, "Where are you?"

He answered, "I heard you in the garden, and I was afraid because I was naked; so I hid.

...The Lord God made garments of skin for Adam and his wife and clothed them. And the Lord God said, "The man has now become like one of us, knowing good and evil. He must not be allowed to reach out his hand and take also from the tree of life and eat, and live forever." So the Lord God banished him from the Garden of Eden to work the ground from which he had been taken.

7 The story of the first sin is well known. Sin began with Adam and Eve, when Eve took and ate the fruit from the tree of the knowledge of good and evil, and then shared the fruit with Adam. Looking back at the quoted language, discuss when shame was first felt by Adam and Eve, and what they did when they felt shame.

_____

_____

_____

_____

_____

8 What did God do to help them with their shame?

_____

_____

_____

_____

_____

9 Even though God helped Adam and Eve with their shame, they still had to live with the consequences of their sin. What were the consequences and how long did they last?

_____

_____

_____

_____

_____

10 Based on the story of Adam and Eve, in what ways do you think that God will help us with our feelings of shame?

_____

_____

_____

_____

_____

11 When God helps us with our shame, will he also eliminate the consequences of our guilty actions or inactions? Discuss why or why not?

_____

_____

_____

_____

_____

Often, as in the "should haves" of life, what we have done wrong was not intentional or was simply done thoughtlessly. Please read about Sarah in Genesis 18:10-15 and Genesis 21:1.

> *Then the Lord said, "I will surely return to you about this time next year, and Sarah your wife will have a son."*
>
> *Now Sarah was listening at the entrance to the tent, which was behind him. Abraham and Sarah were already old and well advanced in years, and Sarah was past the age of childbearing. So Sarah laughed to herself as she thought, "After I am worn out and my master is old, will I now have this pleasure?"*
>
> *Then the Lord said to Abraham, "Why did Sarah laugh and say, 'Will I really have a child, now that I am old?' Is anything too hard for the Lord? I will return to you at the appointed time next year and Sarah will have a son."*
>
> *Sarah was afraid, so she lied and said, "I did not laugh."*
>
> *But he said, "Yes, you did laugh."*
>
> *...Now the Lord was gracious to Sarah as he had said, and the Lord did for Sarah what he had promised.*

12 Sarah was about ninety years old at this time, when she learned that she would become pregnant. Her reaction of laughter was likely a spontaneous response under naturally surprising, and quite unbelievable circumstances. Why do you think she lied when confronted about her laughter?

_____
_____
_____
_____
_____

13 Sarah learned that her reaction of laughter showed a lack of faith in God and his promises. Yet God kept his promise and she had a child about one year later. Discuss how God's response to Sarah was different from God's response to the sins of Adam and Eve.

_____
_____
_____
_____
_____

14 Looking at the final sentence quoted in these passages, why did God keep his promise to Sarah?

_____
_____
_____
_____

Through grace, he kept his promise to Sarah. God helps those whose hearts are fully committed to him. Often we might know of God and believe in him, but we do not sense that we are in a close relationship with God. We can impact that relationship by inviting God into our hearts. He will draw near to us as we draw near to him. Please read James 4:6-10, as printed below.

But he gives us more grace. That is why Scripture says: "God opposes the proud but he gives grace to the humble."

Submit yourselves, then to God. Resist the devil, and he will flee from you. Come near to God and he will come near to you. Wash your hands, you sinners, and purify your hearts, you double-minded. Grieve, mourn and wail. Change your laughter to mourning and your joy to gloom. Humble yourselves before the Lord, and he will lift you up.

15 Looking at this passage, list at least 5 things that someone might do to draw near to God.

_____

_____

_____

_____

_____

16 The language stating that we are to grieve, mourn and wail refers to how we should feel about our sins. Often, when we feel shame, we want to hide our sins as did Adam, Eve and Sarah. What is the difference between grieving and mourning our sins and hiding our sins out of shame?

_____

_____

_____

_____

_____

17 It is clear that God's grace is given to those that humble themselves before the Lord. What does it mean to humble oneself before the Lord? If you have a dictionary, look up the word "humble."

_____

_____

_____

_____

_____

> **Promises to Keep**
>
> For this is what the high and lofty One says—he who lives forever, whose name is Holy; "I live in a high and holy place, but also with him who is contrite and lowly in spirit, to revive the spirit of the lowly and to revive the heart of the contrite. …I have seen his ways, but I will heal him; I will guide him and restore comfort to him."
>
> Isaiah 57:15, 18

Reflection & Encouragement

"To make no mistake is not in the power of man; but from their errors and mistakes the wise and good learn wisdom for the future."

Plutarch

Closing Prayer

Dear Father, thank you for being with us this day. Through your never-ending grace, you help us with our shame and free us from our guilty consciences, just as you have helped Adam, Eve and Sarah. Sometimes we understand our wrongdoings, sometimes we simply act in haste or in ignorance. We thank you for your love and mercy regardless of the circumstances. Rather than hiding from you in our shame, enable us to draw near to you and to know your love for us. We want a full and loving relationship with you. In Jesus' name we pray. Amen.

Week 3 Memory Verse

Let us draw near to God with a sincere heart in full assurance of faith, having our hearts sprinkled to cleanse us from a guilty conscience and having our bodies washed with pure water.

Hebrews 10:22

Homework

❶ Do you have any questions or regrets (i.e., the "what ifs" and "should haves" in life) that have caused you to feel shame? Do you sense that your actions or inactions caused harm or hurt feelings to another person? Identify these regrets, list them in your journal, and write out things you would do differently if the matter were to arise today.

❷ Pray over each of the items identified in question 1 and ask for God to reveal to you any facts or truths that may have been clouded over the years. Pray for his forgiveness for these past mistakes and ask for wisdom enabling you to avoid these and similar mistakes in the future.

❸ In your journal, make a list of changes in your daily or weekly routine that might help you to draw nearer to God (perhaps through Bible reading, prayer time, a devotional book, a group study, volunteer efforts, regular worship participation). I challenge you to identify at least 10 potential changes or new activities that you could consider. Select at least one of these items, through prayer, and work to make it part of your routine.

❹ Please read Week 4 in preparation for the next meeting.

Week 4

Grappling with Guilt

our actions may shame us

Do not be afraid; you will not suffer shame.
Do not fear disgrace; you will not be humiliated.
                                               Isaiah 54:4

Opening Prayer

Dear Lord, our God and Father in Heaven, you have so lavishly loved us and cared for us, in both good times and bad. We thank you for your love, your protection, your uplifting hand, and your guidance in and during all of our trials and difficulties in life. Sometimes we get so caught up in these things that we forget to seek your hand. Forgive us when we allow these times to dishearten us and cause us to doubt your love for us. Today, as we move forward in this Bible study, we pray that you will help us to understand the source and context of our feelings of shame. Give us the strength and courage to face our pasts; help us to understand the truth of our pasts; and enable us to move forward without shame. In Jesus' name we pray. Amen.

Meeting & Greeting

Welcome to our fourth week for the Grapple with Guilt, Shed the Shame covenant group. As we have done in the past, let's again share just a little more about ourselves with each other.

❶ This week, share a childhood story of when you did something for which your parents or teacher punished you. Include in your stories your feelings about the punishment.

Getting Started

❷ In last week's homework, you were given the challenge to identify 10 things that you could potentially do that would help you draw closer to God. Please share one of your ideas with the group, explaining why you liked this particular idea.

_____

_____

_____

_____

_____

Grappling with Guilt—Our Actions May Shame Us

We find ourselves feeling guilty about things that we do or things that we fail to do, which somehow cause harm to another person. We may hurt someone's feelings, cause someone physical harm, destroy a relationship, or damage physical possessions. Most often, we do not intend to cause the harm; but sometimes we know exactly what we are doing. Sometimes we know our actions are wrong or that they will cause harm, and we just don't care enough to make another choice. This section will describe a number of potentially common situations where feelings of guilt or shame have arisen. Volunteers are encouraged to read this piece aloud.

Steve's Story

I was in third grade and we were playing softball in school. I had to run from second base to third base. It was going to be a close play, so I slid into the base with all the speed that I could muster. With my strong sliding motion, I knocked the boy from the other team onto the ground with a thud. He hit hard and began to cry out in pain. He had broken his collar bone. I felt terrible every time that I saw him until he was fully healed. It was my fault! Or was it? Maybe I shouldn't have played so roughly. But I didn't do anything on purpose! I apologized to him and he said that everything was okay; but I always felt like I did something wrong. —Steve

Judi's Story

I was in school, living on an extremely tight budget. In fact, I was going to school full-time, was unemployed, and I had run out of money in my savings account. I was looking for a part-time job, but to no avail. I began charging my groceries to delay the expenses. I sold my car and bought a cheaper one so that I'd have more cash. Still, I found no job. Then, when timing couldn't be worse from a financial perspective, my best friend and past roommate asked me to stand up in her wedding. I wanted to say yes; but I couldn't afford a bridesmaid dress, multiple trips to her hometown, or the costs for a hotel. So I told her no. I tried to explain that I couldn't afford it. She said it was okay and that she'd ask someone else; however, nothing was ever the same after that. I felt awkward attending her wedding, thinking that she was disappointed in me and in our friendship. Eventually, our relationship faded away. I have carried a degree of regret and guilt over that situation ever since, wishing that I had put my friendship ahead of my money matters. —Judi

Sandra's Story

It was a Sunday. The kids and I were invited to go visit a friend and her kids at a swimming pool at a local hotel. My son and daughter were so excited; they immediately got their swimming suits on. In excited anticipation, my daughter became really hyper and started chasing her brother around the house. She tackled him and was wrestling him in the family room while I was trying to relax until it was time to go. I told her four times to settle down because she was being so loud, but she didn't seem to hear me. She has some hearing loss. I finally snapped and yelled really loud, telling her to get her butt upstairs and get clothes on because she wasn't coming to the pool with us. My husband gave me a look like I was going to the extreme-after all, our daughter was just being a kid. Later, she came downstairs to apologize to me with tears in her eyes. I told her she did nothing wrong and that Mommy was just crabby; and I apologized to her. She ended up coming to the pool, and we all had a great time. However, I still feel horrible that I snapped at her for no reason. I hope that she doesn't remember this. —Sandra

George's Story

My parents were heavy smokers. They had this smoking stand that had an ashtray, a couple drink holders and a compartment for holding the new packs of cigarettes. One time when I was in 8th grade, I decided to try smoking; so I took one of the new packs of cigarettes from the stand. My mom noticed that a pack was missing right away that evening, and she instantly accused and angrily questioned my older brother. He, of course, adamantly and truthfully denied having taken the cigarettes. Seeing how much trouble he was going to get into, I decided it was best to just stay quiet and let him take the blame. Mom never suspected that I was the guilty one. —George

> **Promises to Keep**
> You know my folly, O God;
> my guilt is not hidden from you.
> Psalm 69:5

No one is perfect. No one can manage to always do all things correctly. We may do something harmful or hurtful, intentionally or unintentionally, knowingly or unknowingly, or with or without malice. No matter what the circumstances, it is important to grapple with our guilt by understanding the truth of the situation and by accepting appropriate responsibility for our actions.

❸ For each of the above stories, discuss whether the person actually did something wrong or not. Decide who was actually responsible for what happened, and whether he or she acted intentionally or unintentionally.

_____

_____

❹ The author's story about abortion is an example of a choice made without understanding that the choice was wrong, and without understanding the seriousness of its consequences. Please share another example in which someone has done something wrong, but may not understand the seriousness of the matter.

❺ Please share examples of when someone you know either did something wrong, but tried to blame another person, or, as in George's story, allowed someone else to take the blame. For each example, determine the wrongdoing, the harm caused, and the person that was really responsible.

Bible Study

In the last chapter we read about Adam and Eve and the shame that they felt after disobeying God. Please read the following additional verses from Genesis in which we learn a little more about their responses when confronted by God about their wrongdoing. Genesis 3:8-19:

Toward evening they heard the Lord God walking about in the garden, so they hid themselves among the trees. The Lord God called to Adam, "Where are you?"

He replied, "I heard you, so I hid. I was afraid because I was naked."

"Who told you that you were naked?" the Lord God asked. "Have you eaten the fruit I commanded you not to eat?"

"Yes," Adam admitted, "but it was the woman you gave me who brought me the fruit, and I ate it."

Then the Lord God asked the woman, "How could you do such a thing?"

"The serpent tricked me," she replied. "That's why I ate it."

So the Lord God said to the serpent, "Because you have done this, you will be punished. You are singled out from all the domestic and wild animals of the whole earth to be cursed. You will grovel in the dust as long as you live, crawling along on your belly. From now on, you and the woman will be enemies, and your offspring and her offspring will be enemies. He will crush your head, and you will strike his heel."

Then he said to the woman, "You will bear children with intense pain and suffering. And though your desire will be for your husband, he will be your master."

And to Adam he said, "Because you listened to your wife and ate the fruit I told you not to eat, I have placed a curse on the ground. All your life you will struggle to scratch a living from it. It will grow thorns and thistles for you, though you will eat of its grains. All your life you will sweat to produce food, until your dying day. Then you will return to the ground from which you came. For you were made from dust, and to the dust you will return."

6 When confronted by God about eating the forbidden fruit, Adam and Eve both tried to blame someone else for their actions. Who do you feel is the responsible party for their sins? Why?

_____

_____

_____

_____

7 God punished all three of them, Adam, Eve and the serpent. Do you agree that this was a just answer? Why or why not?

Week 4: Grappling with Guilt / 75

_____
_____
_____
_____
_____

❽ Do you think that God's response to this sin would have been any different if Adam or Eve would have simply confessed without trying to shift the blame? Why or why not?

_____
_____
_____
_____
_____

Please read the following story about Cain, who killed his brother out of jealousy. Genesis 4:8-10:

Now Cain said to his brother Abel, "Let's go out to the field." And while they were in the field, Cain attacked his brother Abel and killed him.

Then the Lord said to Cain, "Where is your brother Abel?"

"I don't know," he replied. "Am I my brother's keeper?"

The Lord said, "What have you done? Listen! Your brother's blood cries out to me from the ground. Now you are under a curse and driven from the ground, which opened its mouth to receive your brother's blood from your hand. When you work the ground, it will no longer yield its crops for you. You will be a restless wanderer on the earth."

❾ What did Cain do when God confronted him about killing his brother?

_____
_____
_____
_____
_____

10 Was Cain able to avoid punishment or all other consequences of his action by lying to God?

_____

_____

_____

_____

_____

11 It is common for people to try to avoid punishment by lying or otherwise hiding the evidence of their wrongdoing. If you don't "get caught" by someone in authority, will that ensure that you will not have to face the consequences of your wrongdoing? Why or why not?

_____

_____

_____

_____

_____

> **Promises to Keep**
>
> "His eyes are on the ways of men;
> he sees their every step.
> There is no dark place, no deep shadow,
> where evildoers can hide."
>
> Elihu, Job 34:21-22

Sometimes we are not even aware that we have done something wrong, or we are not aware of the depths of our wrongdoing. Please read the following story about Abraham and Abimelech from Genesis 20:1-7 and 16-17.

Now Abraham moved on from there into the region of the Negev and lived between Kadesh and Shur. For a while he stayed in Gerar, and there Abraham said of his wife Sarah, "She is my sister." Then Abimelech king of Gerar sent for Sarah and took her.

But God came to Abimelech in a dream one night and said to him, "You are as good as dead because of the woman you have taken; she is a married woman."

Now Abimelech had not gone near her, so he said, "Lord, will you destroy an innocent nation? Did he not say to me, 'She is my sister,' and didn't she also say, 'He is my brother'? I have done this with a clear conscience and clean hands."

Then God said to him in the dream, "Yes, I know you did this with a clear conscience, and so I have kept you from sinning against me. That is why I did not let you touch her. Now return the man's wife, for he is a prophet, and he will pray for you and you will live. But if you do not return her, you may be sure that you and all yours will die."

…To Sarah he said, "I am giving your brother a thousand shekels of silver. This is to cover the offense against you before all who are with you; you are completely vindicated."

Then Abraham prayed to God, and God healed Abimelech, his wife and his slave girls so they could have children again, for the Lord had closed up every womb in Abimelech's household because of Abraham's wife Sarah.

12 What does this story tell us about God and how he views intentional wrongdoing as compared to unintentional wrongdoing?

_____

_____

_____

_____

_____

13 In this case, even though Abimelech intended to lay with Sarah, he had not done so before learning that she was actually married to Abraham. Even when acting innocently, what consequences did Abimelech face for his unintentional wrongdoing?

_____

_____

_____

_____

_____

14 What consequences do you think Abimelech would have faced if he did not return Sarah to Abraham once he learned the truth?

_____

_____

_____

_____

_____

Please read the following story about King David, from 2 Samuel 12:1-13.

The Lord sent Nathan to David. When he came to him, he said, "There were two men in a certain town, one rich and the other poor. The rich man had a very large number of sheep and cattle, but the poor man had nothing except one little ewe lamb he had bought. He raised it, and it grew up with him and his children. It shared his food, drank from his cup and even slept in his arms. It was like a daughter to him.

"Now a traveler came to the rich man, but the rich man refrained from taking one of his own sheep or cattle to prepare a meal for the traveler who had come to him. Instead, he took the ewe lamb that belonged to the poor man and prepared it for the one who had come to him."

David burned with anger against the man and said to Nathan, "As surely as the Lord lives, the man who did this deserves to die! He must pay for that lamb four times over, because he did such a thing and had no pity."

Then Nathan said to David, "You are the man! This is what the Lord, the God of Israel, says: 'I anointed you king over Israel, and I delivered you from the hand of Saul. I gave your master's house to you, and your master's wives into your arms. I gave you the house of Israel and Judah. And if all this had been too little, I would have given you even more. Why did you despise the word of the Lord by doing what is evil in his eyes? You struck down Uriah the Hittite with the sword and took his wife to be your own. You killed him with the sword of the Ammonites. Now, therefore, the sword will never depart from your house, because you despised me and took the wife of Uriah the Hittite to be your own.'

"This is what the Lord says: 'Out of your own household I am going to bring calamity upon you. Before your very eyes I will take your wives and give them to the one who is close to you, and he will lie with your wives in broad daylight. You did it in secret, but I will do this thing in broad daylight before all Israel.'"

Then David said to Nathan, "I have sinned against the Lord."

Nathan replied, "The Lord has taken away your sin. You are not going to die."

(15) What sins did King David commit? (See 2 Samuel, chapter 11 for a full account of King David's affair.)

_____
_____
_____
_____
_____

(16) How did God bring King David to understand that he had sinned?

_____
_____
_____
_____
_____

(17) Discuss the various ways that God might use to make us aware that we have sinned.

_____
_____
_____
_____
_____

> **Promises to Keep**
>
> Godly sorrow brings repentance that leads to salvation and leaves no regret, but worldly sorrow brings death.
> 2 Corinthians 7:10

Please read the following verse from Luke 12: 47-48:

> *"That servant who knows his master's will and does not get ready or does not do what his master wants will be beaten with many blows. But the one who does not know and does*

things deserving punishment will be beaten with few blows. From everyone who has been given much, much will be demanded; and from the one who has been entrusted with much, much more will be asked."

18 King David did not seem to fully understand his guilt until Nathan pointed it out to him. Perhaps he thought he had completely hidden his sin by marrying Uriah's wife. Yet, unlike Abimelech, King David was severely punished. How do Jesus' words from Luke 12 explain this difference?

_____

_____

_____

_____

> **Promises to Keep**
> What the wicked dreads will overtake him; what the righteous desire will be granted.
> Proverbs 10:24

Reflection & Encouragement

"We have not passed that subtle line between childhood and adulthood until…we have stopped saying 'It got lost,' and say, 'I lost it.'"

Sydney J. Harris

Closing Prayer

Dear God, our creator and redeemer. In many ways we fail to live our lives as you have commanded us. Sometimes, we don't even recognize our failures. Other times, we may think we are doing the right things, but are still acting in error. Open our eyes and our hearts to your will. Walk with us each day and help us to make choices that honor you, choices that bring ourselves or others closer to you, and choices that are always consistent with your commands. In Jesus' name we pray. Amen.

Week 4 Memory Verse

For all have sinned and fall short of the glory of God, and are justified freely by his grace through the redemption that came by Christ Jesus.

Romans 3:23-24

Homework

1 Pray that God will open your eyes to the ways that you have sinned. Ask him to reveal the errors of your past in ways that will teach you to walk in his ways in the future.

2 In your journal, make a list of ten sins of the past that have caused feelings of shame. Determine the responsibility for each wrong (maybe there is shared responsibility with other people) being careful not to inappropriately blame others. Accept the responsibility when it belongs to you, being careful not to accept blame that truly belongs to others.

3 Pray again over this list, seeking God's forgiveness. Ask him to help you to learn from your past mistakes.

4 Read Week 5 in preparation for the next meeting.

Week 5

I Confess, I Repent

lifting the shame

If we confess our sins, he is faithful and just and will forgive us our sins and purify us from all unrighteousness.

1 John 1:9

Opening Prayer

Dear Holy Father, we thank you for opening our eyes and our hearts to the things that we have done that may have harmed us or others. We want to act according to your will, but we don't always do what is best. Sometimes we choose what seems to be the simplest path rather than what may be the best path. Sometimes we just make mistakes. Other times, the temptation to do wrong overwhelms us. We pray for your presence again today as we learn more about our guilt and shame. Help us understand how we impact those around us. Enable us to treat others with love, as you have loved us. And, dear Lord, when we fail, create in us humble hearts as we confess our sins, repent, and seek your forgiveness. Amen.

Meeting & Greeting

Welcome to our fifth week in the Grapple with Guilt, Shed the Shame covenant group. Thank you for sticking with this study. Last week, we focused on identifying the basis for our shame, and whether that basis is our own doing. This week we will look at God's plan for forgiveness.

❶ Please share a story of a time when you apologized to someone. Add what happened after you apologized and how you felt after doing so.

___

Getting Started

② When doing your homework from last week, did anyone recall a situation involving a feeling of shame that was long ago forgotten?

③ Discuss why God might reveal to us the mistakes or errors of our past, rather than to simply leave them in the past if they have been forgotten.

④ Discuss the difference between assigning responsibility and shifting the blame.

I Confess, I Repent—Lifting the Shame

This section provides examples of how the burden of guilt is often lifted through confession, repentance and forgiveness. Volunteers are encouraged to read this piece aloud.

Terry's Story

When I was a kid, we were very poor. Although I'm not proud of it, I used to take money out of my mother's purse. I always felt ashamed, and I told myself that I'd repay it when I was older and had a job. I always wanted to tell my mother how sorry I was as she must have missed that money. Because I was too ashamed and could never quite figure out how to bring it up for discussion, she died without me ever being able to say that I'm sorry. —Terry

> **Promises to Keep**
>
> When I kept silent, my bones wasted away
> through my groaning all day long.
> For day and night your hand was heavy upon
> me; my strength was sapped
> as in the heat of summer.
>
> Psalm 32:3-4

Brad's Story

It was such a long time ago, now. We were having so much fun. You know how it is. I was out with the boys. Actually, I was out with my brother-in-law. As I tell my wife, I was just trying to get along with her family. Anyway, as the night carried on, I jokingly told my brother-in-law that I really liked a particular picture that was hanging on the wall in the tavern, and that I would pay him twenty dollars if he would steal it for me. I was joking of course, but the conversation got carried away. The next thing I knew, he took the picture off the wall and took it out to my car. The following day, I felt very badly about what we did, so I took the picture back and apologized. The owner of the tavern was very grateful to have his picture back as he had won it as a prize from a special sales promotion. He was so grateful that he thanked me for returning the picture, told me not to worry about it, and invited me to sit down and have a drink with him. I'm glad I did the right thing in the end. I would have felt ashamed every time I went there if I had not returned the picture. I'm not sure I would have even gone back there again if I hadn't made amends. —Brad

> **Promises to Keep**
>
> Then I acknowledged my sin to you and did not cover up my iniquity, I said, "I will confess my transgressions to the Lord" — and you forgave the guilt of my sin.
>
> Psalm 32:5

Joanne's Story

My parents were on a trip and my siblings were at my grandparents' house a half hour drive away. I was a sophomore in high school. My grandparents agreed to let me stay home alone because I had a concert at school the next day. They trusted me. I didn't realize I would hurt my grandmother when I threw a party at my parents' house. Although I was not accustomed to drinking, I invited everyone over for a drinking party. Some of the people that came over were my friends, but many of them were people that just used me for a place to party. Well, the party got way out of hand. It wasn't fun. The house was a mess, a glass table was cracked, and there were eggs on the ceiling!

My parents were so angry when they came home. They grounded me for three months. They also prevented me from seeing certain friends. They even called the school and told the teachers that I was not allowed to speak with these particular friends.

My relationship with my grandparents was hurt for a very long time. My beloved grandfather wouldn't look at me the next few times we were together for family gatherings, except to tell me that I had really hurt my grandmother. I broke her trust. She didn't think I would do that kind of thing. I made her look bad. Apparently, my dad didn't trust the situation before they left home, so he wanted me to stay at my grandparents' home along with my siblings. My grandmother insisted that I could be trusted. I proved that he was right and my grandmother was wrong.

I felt so ashamed.

Eventually, we talked about it more. I said that I was sorry many times. I didn't want them to think of me as a lying kid that couldn't be trusted. I wanted them to trust me again. I worked hard to gain their trust back. I wanted to show my parents and grandparents that I could be a responsible person. It took a long time, but I worked through the guilt and shame and became a better person. Ultimately, my mistake, punishment, and shame benefited me. I'm so thankful that my parents and grandparents cared enough to make sure I knew what I had done was wrong. I felt guilty for my mistakes and I felt shameful for hurting my grandparents; but I worked through the situation to become a better person. —Joanne

> **Promises to Keep**
>
> Repent, then, turn to God, so that your sins may be wiped out, that times of refreshing may come from the Lord.
>
> Psalm 32:5

Bible Study

When we do something wrong, we often feel regret, sorrow or shame. There are two common reasons for this regret or sorrow: one is worldly sorrow due to a fear of getting caught; and the other is godly sorrow which reflects a repentant changed heart. Please read 2 Corinthians 7:10-11.

Godly sorrow brings repentance that leads to salvation and leaves no regret, but worldly sorrow brings death. See what this godly sorrow has produced in you: what earnestness, what eagerness to clear yourselves, what indignation, what alarm, what longing, what concern, what readiness to see justice done.

❺ Compare and contrast the differences between godly sorrow and worldly sorrow.

_____

_____

_____

_____

_____

❻ Looking back to the author's introductory story about her teenage pregnancy and abortion, would you describe her sorrow about the pregnancy as godly sorrow or worldly sorrow? Why?

7 Would you describe the author's sorrow about having chosen abortion as godly sorrow or worldly sorrow? Why? How did her sorrow change over time?

8 In the stories for this week, Terry could never bring himself to tell his mother about stealing the money. Do you think Terry faced worldly sorrow, godly sorrow or both? Please explain.

9 Do you believe that Brad and Joanne felt worldly sorrow or godly sorrow or both? Please explain..

❿ Terry never faced up to his sin. Joanne was caught in her sin. Brad confessed and repented for stealing the picture. Compare and contrast the results or consequences in each case.

_____

_____

_____

_____

_____

If one is truly repentant, that person will change his or her ways. Please read the following excerpts from the story about Manasseh as written in 2 Chronicles 33:1-6, 10-13, and 16.

Manasseh was twelve years old when he became king, and he reigned in Jerusalem fifty-five years. He did evil in the eyes of the Lord, following the detestable practices of the nations the Lord had driven out before the Israelites. He rebuilt the high places his father Hezekiah had demolished; he also erected alters to the Baals and made Asherah poles. He bowed down to all the starry hosts and worshiped them. He built altars in the temple of the Lord, of which the Lord had said, "My Name will remain in Jerusalem forever." In both courts of the temple of the Lord, he built altars to all the starry hosts. He sacrificed his sons in the fire in the Valley of Ben Hinnom, practiced sorcery, divination and witchcraft, and consulted mediums and spiritists. He did much evil in the eyes of the Lord, provoking him to anger.

...The Lord spoke to Manasseh and his people, but they paid no attention. So the Lord brought against them the army commanders of the king of Assyria, who took Manasseh prisoner, put a hook in his nose, bound him with bronze shackles and took him to Babylon. In his distress he sought the favor of the Lord his God and humbled himself greatly before the God of his fathers. And when he prayed to him, the Lord was moved by his entreaty and listened to his plea; so he brought him back to Jerusalem and to his kingdom. Then Manasseh knew that the Lord is God.

...Then he restored the altar of the Lord and sacrificed fellowship offerings and thank offerings on it, and told Judah to serve the Lord, the God of Israel.

⓫ From this story, we don't know exactly what Manasseh said in his prayers when he pleaded with God. Describe what you think Manasseh may have said when he prayed to God.

12 What can we learn from Manasseh's behavior that may serve as a guide for us when we have sinned?

Sometimes when we do something wrong, we may want to seek forgiveness, but our shame overwhelms us or we believe that forgiveness is too much to ask. Perhaps this is what Terry felt when he could not admit that he stole from his mother. Please read Luke 7:36-48, as printed below, to learn what Jesus has to say about forgiveness and the magnitude of our sins.

Now one of the Pharisees invited Jesus to have dinner with him, so he went to the Pharisee's house and reclined at the table. When a woman who had lived a sinful life in that town learned that Jesus was eating at the Pharisee's house, she brought an alabaster jar of perfume, and as she stood behind him at his feet weeping, she began to wet his feet with her tears. Then she wiped them with her hair, kissed them and poured perfume on them.

When the Pharisee who had invited him saw this, he said to himself, "If this man were a prophet, he would know who is touching him and what kind of woman she is - that she is a sinner."

Jesus answered him, "Simon, I have something to tell you."

"Tell me, teacher," he said.

"Two men owed money to a certain moneylender. One owed him five hundred denarii, and the other fifty. Neither of them had the money to pay him back, so he canceled the debts of both. Now which of them will love him more?"

Simon replied, "I suppose the one who had the bigger debt canceled."

"You have judged correctly," Jesus said.

Then he turned toward the woman and said to Simon, "Do you see this woman? I came into your house. You did not give me any water for my feet, but she wet my feet with her tears and wiped them with her hair. You did not give me a kiss, but this woman, from the time I entered, has not stopped kissing my feet. You did not put oil on my head, but she has poured perfume on my feet. Therefore, I tell you, her many sins have been forgiven - for she loved much. But he who has been forgiven little loves little."

Then Jesus said to her, "Your sins are forgiven."

13 Regarding the parable of the two debtors, which debtor is the woman in this story most like? Why?

_____

_____

_____

_____

_____

14 Describe the feelings of the woman's heart when she came to Jesus.

_____

_____

_____

_____

_____

15 Based on this story, what do you feel Jesus is telling us about God's forgiveness?

_____

_____

_____

_____

_____

> **Promises to Keep**
>
> Everyone who calls on the name of the Lord will be saved.
>
> Romans 10:13

16 Repentance is based on a changed heart and it results in changed behavior. Discuss the comparison that Jesus made between the woman and Simon, the Pharisee. Which one of these people do you believe is likely to change the most following this encounter with Jesus? Why?

_____

_____

_____

_____

_____

Reflection & Encouragement

"[Shep] once made a mistake and barked savagely at an old friend. ... Later, as we all sat in the yard, he seemed uneasy. ... At last he walked deliberately to the visitor, sat up, and held out his paw. It was so plainly an apology that our friend said: 'That's all right, Shep, old fellow! Shake and forget it!' Shep shook hands and walked away perfectly satisfied."

Laura Ingalls Wilder

"Repentance means being sorry enough for our sin to stop; convicted enough by our sin to turn from it; broken enough by our sin to be willing to change."

Roy Lessin

Closing Prayer

Today's closing prayer is adapted from the prayer written by King David after he committed adultery with Bathsheba. The original language in the Bible can be found in Psalm 51:1-6 and 10-12.

Have mercy on us today, O God, according to your unfailing love; according to your great compassion blot out our transgressions. Wash away all our iniquities and cleanse us from our sin.

We know our transgressions, and our sin is always before us. Against you, we have sinned. We have done what is evil in your sight, so that you are proved right when you speak and justified when you judge. Surely we were sinful at birth, sinful from the time our mothers conceived us. Surely you desire truth in the inner parts, and you teach us wisdom in the inmost place.

Create in us pure hearts, O God, and renew in each of us a steadfast spirit. Do not cast us from your presence. Do not take your Holy Spirit from us. Restore to each of us the joy of your salvation and grant us a willing spirit, to sustain us.

Seeking your loving mercy and forgiveness, we confess to you the sins of our hearts, and we thank you for your everlasting grace. Amen

Week 5 Memory Verse

There is rejoicing in the presence of the angels of God over one sinner who repents.

Luke 15:10

Homework

1. Review the list of mistakes, errors or sins that you made as part of your homework last week. For each item, decide whether you felt badly about it out of godly sorrow or out of worldly sorrow.

2. For each item on the list, determine who may have been harmed by your behavior. Then write a short paragraph of apology to each person that may have been harmed, asking him or her for forgiveness. (Do not deliver the written apology to the person.)

3. If you are aware that a particular matter is not resolved between both you and the person once harmed by your actions, pray for God's guidance on whether or not it would be right to discuss the situation with the affected person. (Sometimes it is best to leave a past mistake in the past, as bringing it up would serve no positive purpose for the person once harmed.)

④ As is taught in the powerful fifth step for Alcoholics Anonymous, it is healing to admit to God, to ourselves and to another human being the exact nature of our actions. If you are unable to confess to the person that you may have harmed, consider confessing to another person, such as your pastor or priest, or a loved one.

⑤ Please read Week 6 in preparation for the next meeting.

Week 6

I Am Forgiven!

and reconciled to God

Therefore, there is now no condemnation for those who are in Christ Jesus, because through Christ Jesus the law of the Spirit of life sets me free from the law of sin and death.

Romans 8:1-2

Opening Prayer

Dear Lord, our Father, thank you for loving us and keeping us as your children. We thank you for reconciling us to you through your son, Jesus Christ. Bless us today with your presence as we work through this Bible study. Open our eyes and our hearts so that we can see how we have failed you, those that we love, and all others. With open and repentant hearts, we come to you for your forgiveness. Strengthen our faith in Jesus Christ so that we will not only know of your forgiveness, but that we will be able to accept your forgiveness. Thank you, dear Father. Amen.

Meeting & Greeting

Welcome to our sixth week for the Grapple with Guilt, Shed the Shame covenant group. Thank you again for sharing your time with each other today.

❶ Today, please tell us a story about a pet and how that pet showed love to its owner.

_____

_____

_____

Getting Started

2 In your homework, you were asked to write an apology to those on your list that you have hurt through either an action or inaction. The homework specifically stated that you should not send the apology. Discuss why it might not be a good idea to rush out and apologize to someone.

_____

_____

_____

_____

3 Discuss the healing impact of confessing to God, to oneself and to another human being. Why would confessing to another human being be helpful?

_____

_____

_____

_____

4 In an episode of the television sitcom called "Becker", an old friend of Dr. Becker's showed up after several years to confess all the rotten things that he had done to Dr. Becker when he was in medical school. Dr. Becker did not know that his friend had done these things in the past, and became quite angry with him upon hearing the confessions. Confessing and apologizing are good things to do when done for the right reasons; but sometimes, when done for the wrong reasons, confessing can cause harm. Please describe when confession might result in more harm than good.

_____

_____

_____

_____

_____

> **Promises to Keep**
>
> And the prayer offered in faith will make the sick person well. The Lord will raise him up. If he has sinned, he will be forgiven. Therefore, confess your sins to each other and pray for each other so that you may be healed.
>
> James 5:15-16

I Am Forgiven...And Reconciled to God

This section provides examples of how we carry our shame for a very long time, often for years, because we are unable to obtain forgiveness from the person or people that we have hurt. However, in faith, we can know that we are forgiven by God and with him we are reconciled, regardless of our ability to find reconciliation with the person that we hurt. Again, volunteers are encouraged to read this piece aloud.

Kelly's Story

I will feel horrible if my dad should die and we have not yet straightened this out. I keep trying to approach him, but he refuses to speak to me. It all started with my dad's bankruptcy and divorce. One of my best friends is coincidentally married to my stepmother's son (my stepbrother). My dad expects me to end this friendship, since he is divorcing my stepmother. He claims that by continuing this friendship, I am supporting his ex-wife over him. He even told me that he wants me to be unhappy and miserable if I continue this relationship. Recently he returned a birthday card that I had sent. The card was ripped into pieces. He included a note saying that I should stop wasting my money as he doesn't want to hear from me. Now, I wonder what he has said to the rest of the family. Recently, I was visiting my eighty-nine year old grandmother when my dad's sister called. I answered the phone. When she learned that I was on the phone, her voice turned cold, as she abruptly ended the conversation. Later, I learned that the entire family held a birthday celebration for my grandmother, and I wasn't invited. I don't know how to make amends without giving in to his unreasonable demands. I feel very badly, but I'm not the one that is wrong. —Kelly

Christine's Story

Seven years after my father died, it finally hit me; and it hit hard. I was talking to the pastor at our church when I finally broke into tears, as I relayed to him that I felt shame all this time because I didn't go home for Thanksgiving. My son was young and he had an ear infection. It just didn't make sense to take him out in the cold and drive to my dad's for Thanksgiving. So I canceled on short notice. I thought it wouldn't matter that much, because I knew I'd see him in just a month for Christmas. How was I to know that he was going to have a heart attack and die just two weeks later? There's so much I wish I could have said to him before he died. If only I had gone to see him over Thanksgiving. —Christine

Amy's Story

When I was in college, I often babysat for my aunt's three boys. The oldest was fifteen years old and the others were ten and eleven years old. The last time that I babysat for them was when my aunt and uncle took a weekend vacation. I also needed to work at my part-time job on Saturday afternoon. I thought it would be okay to leave the boys alone for an afternoon. The oldest was clearly old enough to take care of the others for a few hours. When I got back from work, the house looked in order and the oldest boy had made dinner. The rest of the weekend went well, and I left Sunday night when my aunt and uncle returned home. Monday morning my uncle called me on the telephone to ask where his truck was. I was dumbfounded! It had been in the garage, but since I never checked the garage, I didn't know it was gone! I felt like the worst babysitter ever! As the tale unwound, we found out that the oldest boy and the neighbor kid had taken it for a joy ride in a nearby farm field Saturday afternoon while I had gone to work. It now had a broken axle. The boys never told me. My aunt and uncle said that they forgave me and didn't hold me responsible. But I'm not so sure about that. They have never asked me to babysit for them again. We don't ever talk about it any more. —Amy

Joe's Story

I didn't mean to hurt them. I just wasn't thinking. I know that it is illegal to drive drunk. I know better. I just went out with the guys after work for a couple drinks during "Happy Hour." I apparently had more than I realized. We all left the bar at the same time. I headed west. There was a lot of traffic. I guess I was distracted or something. Heck, I don't know. Suddenly, without time enough to react, the car in front of me put on its brakes to make a turn. My truck slammed into their trunk. We hit hard. The car in front jolted forward and spun out of control. It was totaled. The little girls in the back seat were hurt. The ambulances took them away. I later learned that their injuries resulted in permanent brain damage. I ruined their lives forever. I'm scum. Apologies won't help. Nothing can help. —Joe

The above examples may be common to the life events that many of us either know about or share. Continuing down the spectrum of seriousness, the author's story of abortion is a situation involving the death of her baby. There will be no opportunity for the author to obtain forgiveness from and reconciliation with her baby during this lifetime. She must live with the consequences of her choice forever.

Some people intentionally commit crimes, such as murder. Consider the example in Charles "Tex" Watson. Watson was the right hand man to Charlie Manson, who was the mastermind behind the gruesome, 1969 murder of Sharon Tate and four others at the Tate home. Sharon Tate was eight and a half months pregnant at the time. Watson was one of the murderers. Once on death row until the death penalty was abolished in 1972 and still in prison for these murders and others, Watson has tried to apologize to the families of his victims, noting that he lives with remorse and shame every day. How is it possible for these families to forgive him?[1]

For whatever the reason, there may be no way to obtain forgiveness from someone that we have hurt, and there may be no way to reconcile with them, regardless of the degree of our guilt. As a result, it is often very hard to shed the shame that develops in our hearts. But always know that God can and will forgive you, and that he will reconcile you to him. With God, you have a complete relationship built on his love and grace. As difficult as it may be to believe, even Charles

"Tex" Watson has found peace through the grace and forgiveness of our Lord Jesus Christ.[2]

Whatever is the extent of your guilt and resultant shame, know that God's love is bigger than your sin. Jesus can and will forgive you.

> **Promises to Keep**
>
> Though your sins are like scarlet,
> they shall be as white as snow;
> though they are red as crimson,
> they shall be like wool.
>
> Isaiah 1:18

5 Kelly's father believes that Kelly has wronged him. Kelly believes that her father's demands are unreasonable. Discuss how reconciliation might be possible when neither person is willing to "give in."

_____
_____
_____
_____
_____

6 Looking at Christine's story, who did she believe that she hurt? Why do you think it took her so many years to find closure for this situation?

_____
_____
_____
_____
_____

7 Amy isn't sure that her aunt and uncle have forgiven her. Why not? Do you think that she should do anything more about it now? Explain your reasons.

_____

8 God forgives even what seems unforgivable. Discuss how God's forgiveness can give us peace.

> **Promises to Keep**
> "All the prophets testify about him that everyone who believes in him receives forgiveness of sins through his name."
> Acts 10:43

Bible Study

Judas sought forgiveness for betraying Jesus, but it seems that he didn't know what to do to find forgiveness. Please have someone read Matthew 27, verses 3-5, as written below.

When Judas, who had betrayed him, saw that Jesus was condemned, he was seized with remorse and returned the thirty silver coins to the chief priests and the elders. "I have sinned," he said, "for I have betrayed innocent blood."

"What is that to us?" they replied. "That's your responsibility."

So Judas threw the money into the temple and left. Then he went away and hanged himself.

9 Judas felt remorse, and tried to correct his wrongdoing. So he returned to the chief priests and confessed. They did not help him. They also did nothing to help Jesus. In fact, they laid all responsibility on Judas. Out of despair, Judas hanged himself. What do you think would have happened if Judas had gone to Jesus and confessed?

❿ Would confession to Jesus have changed the outcome (crucifixion of Christ) of Judas' initial betrayal? Why or why not.

⓫ If you cannot change the outcome of your wrongdoing, why then would you or should you confess?

In Week 5, we read about a woman who had lived a sinful life. She went to the Pharisee's house, and began weeping, wetting Jesus' feet with her tears and wiping them with her hair. Some of this story is repeated below (to refresh your memory) along with a few additional verses. Please have a volunteer read it aloud. Luke 7:36-38, 49-50:

> *Now one of the Pharisees invited Jesus to have dinner with him, so he went to the Pharisee's house and reclined at the table. When a woman who had lived a sinful life in that town learned that Jesus was eating at the Pharisee's house, she brought an alabaster jar of perfume, and as she stood behind him at his feet weeping, she began to wet his feet with her tears. Then she wiped them with her hair, kissed them and poured perfume on them.*
>
> *...Then Jesus said to her, "Your sins are forgiven."*

The other guests began to say among themselves, "Who is this who even forgives sins?"

Jesus said to the woman, "Your faith has saved you; go in peace."

❷ According to Jesus, what saved the woman?

_____

_____

_____

_____

_____

❸ How did the woman exhibit her faith in this story?

_____

_____

_____

_____

As we discussed during Week 4, 2 Samuel, chapter 11 tells the story of King David and his affair with Bathsheba while her husband, Uriah, was away at war. Bathsheba got pregnant from this affair. In attempt to hide the affair, King David brought Uriah back from the war hoping that he would lay with his wife, but he was too loyal to his duties and thus refused to leave the palace. Then to hide the affair, King David sent Uriah back to the war and ordered that he be placed on the front lines of battle, where it was certain that he would be killed. In spite of these sins David was described as a man after God's own heart. See Acts 13:22. Please read the following passage from the Book of Titus, chapter 3: 3-7:

At one time we too were foolish, disobedient, deceived and enslaved by all kinds of passions and pleasures. We lived in malice and envy, being hated and hating one another. But when the kindness and love of God our Savior appeared, he saved us, not because of righteous things we had done, but because of his mercy. He saved us through the washing of rebirth and renewal by the Holy Spirit, whom he poured out on us generously through Jesus Christ our Savior, so that having been justified by his grace, we might become heirs having hope of eternal life.

104 / Grapple with Guilt

14 How does this passage help us to understand God's forgiveness of seemingly unforgivable sins like those of King David?

_____

_____

_____

_____

_____

15 Please summarize what we have learned about the saving grace of God, in light of the stories of Judas and his inability to obtain forgiveness from the chief priests, the sinful woman at the Pharisee's home whose faith saved her, and King David who, even after having a man killed, was still described as a man after God's own heart.

_____

_____

_____

_____

_____

Without forgiveness, our sins often break our relation ships with those that we have hurt. Our sins can also break our relationship with God. But God has provided a path for reconciliation with him. Please read the following Bible passages on the path for reconciliation. Colossians 1:21-23:

Once you were alienated from God and were enemies in your minds because of your evil behavior. But now he has reconciled you by Christ's physical body through death to present you holy in his sight, without blemish and free from accusation - if you continue in your faith, established and firm, not moved from the hope held out in the gospel. This is the gospel that you have heard and that has been proclaimed to every creature under heaven, and of which I, Paul, have become a servant.

2 Corinthians 5:16-21:

So from now on we regard no one from a worldly point of view. Though we once regarded Christ in this way, we do so no longer. Therefore, if anyone is in Christ, he is a new creation; the old has gone, the new has come! All this is from God, who reconciled us to himself through Christ and gave us the ministry of reconciliation; that God was reconciling the world to himself in Christ not counting men's sins against them. And he has committed to us the message of reconciliation. We are therefore Christ's ambassadors, as though God were making his appeal through us. We implore you on Christ's behalf: Be reconciled to God. God made him who had no sin to be sin for us, so that in him we might become the righteousness of God.

16 How did God reconcile us to him?

_____

_____

_____

_____

_____

17 According to the passage quoted from Colossians, is there anyone that God does not want to be reconciled to him?

_____

_____

_____

_____

_____

18 It is often difficult to look at a person (such as Charles "Tex" Watson) that has done something horrendous and see anything but the sin. We often see that person only from a worldly point of view. What do these passages say happens to a person that has been reconciled to God?

_____

_____

_____

_____

_____

> **Promises to Keep**
>
> When you were dead in your sins and in the uncircumcision of your sinful nature, God made you alive with Christ. He forgave us all our sin.
>
> Colossians 2:13

Reflection & Encouragement

"Faith means not only believing God's truth, but trusting Christ, taking what he offers, and then triumphing in the knowledge of what is now yours."

J. I. Packer

Closing Prayer

Our Father, your mercy knows no bounds. Thank you for reconciling us to you, through the saving grace of your son, Jesus Christ. Even when our failings and faults are great, your love and mercy are greater still. Thank you for loving us, accepting us and forgiving us. Be with us throughout each day as we continue along our journey, developing a greater understanding of what brings us shame and how, through you, we may shed that shame. We pray in Jesus' name. Amen.

Week 6 Memory Verse

In him we have redemption through his blood, the forgiveness of sins, in accordance with the riches of God's grace.

Ephesians 1:7

Homework

 Review the letters of apology written as part of your homework for last week. If you were to apologize in person, would the apology help the person that you feel you may have hurt, or would the apology tend to cause more harm? Why?

_____

_____

_____

❷ Are there any cases in which you have not been forgiven by or reconciled to someone that you hurt, either intentionally or unintentionally?

_____

_____

_____

_____

_____

❸ List all reasons that have prevented forgiveness and reconciliation. Pray over this list, seeking God's forgiveness, and the guidance of his Holy Spirit in order that you may find peace.

_____

_____

_____

_____

_____

❹ Add a prayer to your journal asking God to help you to grow in your faith in him and his son, Jesus Christ, so that through such faith you will know that he has forgiven you.

❺ Read Week 7 in preparation for next week's meeting.

Notes

1. Watson, Charles. Manson's Right-Hand Man Speaks Out! Abounding Love Ministries, Inc, 2003. June 26, 2006. <http://www.aboundinglove.org/web2printer/web2printer4.php>.

2. Watson, Tex (i.e., as told to Ray Hoekstra). Will You Die For Me? Crossroads Publications, Inc., 1978. <http://www.aboundinglove.org/sensational/sen-007.php>.

Week 7

But I'm Angry!

must I forgive?

Bless those who persecute you; bless and do not curse.

Romans 12:14

Opening Prayer

O God, our Father, our creator and our redeemer. Again we are meeting as a group to study your Word as it relates to our shame. We thank you for your grace and your gift of forgiveness, given to us through our faith in Jesus Christ and his death and resurrection. We have done things in our pasts that we regret. For many of these things, we have been unable to confess, repent and find reconciliation with the person or persons that we hurt. However, for all of these things, we know that we can trust in your mercy, as we confess to you, ourselves and others. Thank you, dear Father, for reconciling us to you. Help us to change our behaviors so that we will at all times honor you. We pray in Jesus' name. Amen.

Meeting & Greeting

Welcome to the seventh week in our Grapple with Guilt, Shed the Shame covenant group. As we have begun each session, please share another story about yourself.

❶ Tell us a particularly happy memory that you have regarding a family event or vacation.

_____

_____

_____

_____

_____

Getting Started

2 Discuss why we often find it hard to confess our mistakes and then apologize.

_____

_____

_____

_____

_____

3 Discuss the reasons why some people refuse to accept another's apology, or reasons why someone might refuse to forgive another person.

_____

_____

_____

_____

_____

Must I Forgive? You Caused My Shame

This section looks at the ways that we develop feelings of shame resulting from the things that others do to us or the situations that they put us in. Often, the one causing the shameful feelings is either someone in authority or someone that we love, or someone that we believe we are supposed to love. Again, volunteers are encouraged to read this piece aloud.

Becky's Story

I was actually physically sick for a few months every time I walked into work, because of this situation. I felt so isolated. I had been ordered not to speak to anyone in the company about what was going on. If I confided in anyone or tried to discuss it with anyone, I was told I'd be fired.

It all started when I got a new boss. Now I've had many new bosses over my career, but none like this one. She mistreated me right from the start, perhaps because I had been one of the contenders for the job that she now had. First, she took away most of my projects, so that I had almost no work to do. Then, when I had only two remaining projects, I went to her and to her boss to let them know that I had the time and the desire to do more work. The very next day, my workload was reduced to one project. In addition to the workload reduction, there was constant negative feedback. It seemed that everything I did was wrong in her eyes. Finally, on a particularly stressful day due to my father's illness (the status of which my boss was aware), I was called into the conference room and told that I'd be terminated the next day if I did not have an acceptable corrective action plan for my poor work habits. Specifically, I was told that I talked with my hands, that I failed to take initiative and that I asked two questions during a recent meeting. I didn't dare defend myself. I wrote out the required corrective action plan; and, when I turned it in, I requested a mediator. Ultimately, they hired a mediator and nothing more was said about the corrective action plan. Shortly after that, I found a new job.

It took me months to fully get over the feelings of anger and shame regarding that work situation. I was so angry, not so much about what my boss had done to me, but rather how her actions caused me to continually question myself and my abilities. Her accusations seemed so unfounded; yet I could not seem to overcome them. I'm sure that everyone noticed the difference in my work opportunities and in how she was treating me. It angered me and it humiliated me. —Becky

Jason's Story

I can never seem to please her. I feel like I have to walk on eggshells. Without warning, she gets so angry with me. She accuses me of failing to keep a good job, of never providing enough money for our expenses, of never picking up the house, of not picking up the house correctly, of perpetually being disorganized, of never giving her enough attention…. *Oh, what's the use. It is always something.* I can never do anything right in her eyes. Usually, I never even realize that I'm doing something wrong until she blows up. Sometimes I never understand what I did to make her mad. She just says something like, "You should know what you did wrong." She gets mad, grabs the baby and storms into the bedroom, slamming the door. Then I hear her telling the baby what an awful dad and provider I am. Sometimes I hear her calling her mother and saying what a lazy excuse of a husband I am. She even accuses me of things that I never did. Maybe she's right. I try hard, but it is never enough for her. I love her and I want us to be a happy family; but I can't do everything the way she expects all of the time. Half of the time, I can't even figure out what I'm supposed to do to make her happy. Maybe she's right. Maybe I'm not a good father or husband. —Jason

Jennifer's Story

I'm so dirty. I'm just…used merchandise. Who could want me now? Who will ever want me? My thoughts followed me for many years after the abuse. For six years he did this to me. He calls himself my father! I think of him with disgust! I wanted to be protected. I remember begging my mother whenever she left the house to take me with her. "Please take me along," I'd plead. But then she'd go without me. I'd be alone in that house. She didn't know what was happening to me. Maybe she didn't want to know what he was doing to me. I was afraid to tell her. I saw what he did to her, the bruises and the black eyes. He threatened me with the same if I ever said anything. How is a young girl to fight back? At least I could not get pregnant. Thank God that womanhood was a slow arrival for me. The dirtiness and the shame followed me into my first marriage. I sought counseling, which helped some. But I had married too soon. I knew he wasn't the right person for me; but I was just so relieved and thankful that someone would take me, even with my past. I just wanted to be normal. —Jennifer

It can happen in so many ways. We can feel embarrassed, shameful, or worthless by what others have done to us. Mistreatment, constant degrading, or physical or emotional abuse can cause us to question our value, question our worth or our abilities. Sometimes this happens at work, when a boss belittles an employee. It may happen within a marriage, when one spouse criticizes the other over and over again, demanding perfection and belittling him or her for everything that he or she does that is less than perfect. Then, too, it can happen in cases of rape, sexual abuse, child abuse, or other forms of serious, personal violations. The result is shame-shame that is imposed on us by others. Shame that is undeserved, yet felt in the depths of one's core just the same. If you are currently in an abusive situation, I encourage you to take immediate steps to get help. Perhaps a good starting point is a Christian marriage counselor or the pastor or priest of your church. Maybe you need to find a safe haven for battered spouses. There are places of safety, very likely in or near your community. Seek help from someone that you trust. Whatever the situation, get help and take heart in the fact that God will stand by you.

❹ Please share other examples in which a person would likely develop a sense of shame based on the things that another person did to him or her.

_____

_____

_____

_____

_____

❺ Why do you think people develop feelings of shame from the things that others do to them?

_____

_____

_____

_____

_____

> **Promises to Keep**
>
> Doing an injury puts you below your enemy; revenging one makes you but even with him; forgiving it sets you above him.
>
> Benjamin Franklin

Bible Study

God protects us and stands by us when we are in trouble. Please read Psalm 91, as printed below.

*He who dwells in the shelter of the Most High
will rest in the shadow of the Almighty.
I will say of the Lord, "He is my refuge and my fortress,
my God, in whom I trust."
Surely he will save you from the fowler's snare
and from the deadly pestilence.
He will cover you with his feathers,
and under his wings you will find refuge;
his faithfulness will be your shield and rampart.
You will not fear the terror of night,
nor the arrow that flies by day,
nor the pestilence that stalks in the darkness,
nor the plague that destroys at midday.
A thousand may fall at your side,
ten thousand at your right hand,
but it will not come near you.
You will only observe with your eyes
and see the punishment of the wicked.*

*If you make the Most High your dwelling -
even the Lord, who is my refuge -
then no harm will befall you,
no disaster will come near your tent.
For he will command his angels concerning you
to guard you in all your ways;
they will lift you up in their hands,
so that you will not strike your foot against a stone
You will tread upon the lion and the cobra;
you will trample the great lion and the serpent.*

*"Because he loves me" says the Lord, "I will rescue him;
I will protect him, for he acknowledges my name.
He will call upon me, and I will answer him;
I will be with him in trouble,
I will deliver him and honor him.
With long life will I satisfy him and show him my salvation"*

❻ There is no guarantee that we will not face trouble in our lives. However, according to this Psalm, when we face trouble, if we call on the Lord and put our faith in him, what will he do for us?

_____

_____

_____

_____

_____

❼ Notice the clause, "If you make the Most High your dwelling -". List things that you might do to make the Most High your dwelling.

_____

_____

_____

_____

Anger, hatred and revenge are all common reactions to those that have hurt us. It is okay to be angry. Even Jesus showed anger (See John 2:13-17). Please read the following verses about anger and revenge and forgiveness.

Ephesians 4:26-27:

"In your anger, do not sin": Do not let the sun go down while you are still angry, and do not give the devil a foothold.

Proverbs 20:22

Do not say, "I'll pay you back for this wrong!" Wait for the Lord, and he will deliver you.

Romans 12:17-19

Do not repay anyone evil for evil. Be careful to do what is right in the eyes of everybody. If it is possible, as far as it depends on you, live at peace with everyone. Do not take revenge, my friends, but leave room for God's wrath, for it is written: "It is mine to avenge; I will repay," says the Lord.

Ephesians 4:31-32

Get rid of all bitterness, rage and anger, brawling and slander, along with every form of malice. Be kind and compassionate to one another, forgiving each other, just as in Christ God forgave you.

Colossians 3:12-13

Therefore, as God's chosen people, holy and dearly loved, clothe yourselves with compassion, kindness, humility, gentleness and patience. Bear with each other and forgive whatever grievances you may have against one another. Forgive as the Lord forgave you."

Proverbs 25:21-22

*If your enemy is hungry, feed him;
if he is thirsty, give him something to drink.
In doing this, you will heap burning coals on his head,
and the Lord will reward you.*

8 When someone hurts us, it is okay to be angry. According to the verses quoted above, describe the things that we should and should not do when we are angry.

_____

_____

_____

_____

_____

9 If we take revenge or repay evil with evil when we are angry, who is really influencing our lives?

_____

_____

_____

_____

_____

10 The verses from Ephesians suggest that we forgive the wrongdoer. Based on the Bible passages quoted above, what does forgiveness look like?

_____

_____

_____

_____

_____

According to the New International Bible Dictionary, the word forgiveness means "giving up resentment or claim to requital on account of an offense."[1] Requital is compensation or retaliation. Therefore, forgiveness means that we stop demanding payback, revenge, debt or compensation for the wrongdoing.

11 Does this definition of forgiveness change your answer to question 10?

_____

_____

_____

_____

_____

12 If we stop demanding payback, revenge, debt or compensation, will the person ever "pay" for their wrongdoing? Explain. (Particularly look to the verses from Proverbs 20 and Romans 12, as quoted above.)

_____

_____

_____

_____

_____

> **Promises to Keep**
>
> There is no revenge so complete as forgiveness.
>
> Josh Billings

Please read the following additional Bible passages on forgiveness.

Jesus - Luke 17:3-4:

"If your brother sins, rebuke him, and if he repents, forgive him. If he sins against you seven times in a day, and seven times comes back to you and says, 'I repent,' forgive him."

Matthew 18:21-22:

Then Peter came to Jesus and asked, "Lord, how many times shall I forgive my brother when he sins against me? Up to seven times?" Jesus answered, "I tell you, not seven times, but seventy-seven times."

Jesus—Matthew 6:14-15:

"For if you forgive men when they sin against you, your heavenly Father will also forgive you. But if you do not forgive men their sins, your Father will not forgive your sins."

13 Some Bible translations state that Jesus said in Matthew 18 that we are to forgive our brother as often as seventy times seven, or 490 times. Discuss whether Jesus was trying to limit our forgiveness or suggest that we are to forgive so often that we could not count the number.

_____
_____
_____
_____
_____

14 In Luke 17, Jesus said we should forgive if the person repents. Discuss what we might do, then, if the person does not repent.

_____
_____
_____
_____
_____

15 As it states in Ephesians 4, we are not to let the sun go down on our anger. Discuss ways to forgive in our hearts, when there is no repentance by the other person or where direct forgiveness and reconciliation are not possible.

_____
_____

_____

_____

_____

> **Promises to Keep**
>
> Praise be to the Lord, to God our Savior, who daily bears our burdens.
>
> Psalm 68:19

Reflection & Encouragement

Forgiveness Is Sweet

It was so hard to forgive
those who hurt and did me wrong,
the ones who lied, and those who tried
to snuff out my victor's song.

I took the shame and sorrow
they heaped upon my soul,
I bent and broke in pieces,
no longer strong and whole.

My self esteem was zero,
I felt worthless, stained with dirt,
I bowed beneath the burden,
unsure, defamed, and hurt.

But then I met the Savior,
and saw the way He came
to mankind meek and lowly,
shaped of a different frame;

Earthly beauty did not matter,
neither wealth nor fame,
but just to please the Father,
this man with God's own name.

I took His life unto me,
gave Him what had been mine,
I no longer had to worry
if men were cruel or unkind.

I asked for His forgiveness,
and shared it with those in need
of forgiveness for their mortal selves,
for sinful word or deed.

As I granted this Grace, forgiveness,
I gained a blessed relief,
my spirit grew strong with honor,
my heart grew full of peace.

I now seek only God's opinion;
Is He pleased with me?
For He alone is worthy
to judge and demand a change in me.

Joyce Guy²

Closing Prayer

Dear Lord God. We thank you for your never ending grace, and we know that we need to treat those that have hurt us with grace as well. It is so difficult to let go of our pain and our desire for revenge. Help us to find it in our hearts to forgive those that have hurt us. When we feel we are unable to forgive, enable us to lay our sinful desires of anger, hate and revenge at your feet, and let go. When we find forgiveness in our hearts, we trust that you will forgive us for all our sins, and that you will reward us with the healing power of your love. Thank you for understanding how difficult forgiveness is for us. Thank you for hearing our prayers. Thank you for healing our pain and our shame. Amen.

Week 7 Memory Verse

Don't let evil get the best of you, but conquer evil by doing good.

Romans 12:21 (NLT)

Homework

 Look again at Psalm 91, which has numerous clauses about ways that God will protect you. Pick one that gives you the most comfort and write it in your journal. Try to picture yourself in a difficult situation. Then picture God helping you in this manner.

❷ There are many stories about sin and forgiveness in the Bible. Read the story about Joseph and his jealous brothers, who sold him into slavery, in Genesis chapter 37. Then read about how Joseph forgave his brothers several years later in Genesis 45:4-15.

❸ Is there someone in your life that has hurt you that you have not forgiven? Write about the situation in your journal. Ask God to help you to forgive him or her in the same way that God has forgiven you. If forgiveness does not seem possible at this time, give the issue to God, tell him it is too great for you to bear, and ask him to relieve you of this burden.

_____

_____

_____

_____

_____

❹ Read Week 8 in preparation for next week's meeting.

Notes

1. Tenney, Merrill C., ed. *New International Bible Dictionary: Based on the NIV.* Grand Rapids, MI: Zondervan, 1987.

2. Reprinted with Permission. Joyce Guy of Milton, Florida.

Week 8

Jesus Knows Your Pain

everyone is against me!

"I have told you these things, so that in me you may have peace. In this world you will have trouble. But take heart! I have overcome the world."

Jesus, John 16:33

Opening Prayer

We come to you again, this day, dear Father in heaven to praise you for your greatness. Only you can truly bear the burdens of this world. Through you, however, we know that we will have the strength to bear our own burdens, even the burdens of anger and shame created by those that have hurt us, no matter how severely. The harm done by others comes from the evil in this world; but you are stronger than the evil forces of this world. Through you, we too are stronger than such evil forces. Thank you for putting your loving arms around us. Thank you for your daily support. Thank you for continually coming to our rescue when we are in harm's way. Amen.

Meeting & Greeting

Welcome to our eighth week for the Grapple with Guilt, Shed the Shame covenant group. To open the conversation today, please tell each other a little more about yourselves.

❶ Please share a story of a time when you did not feel like you fit in with the rest of the crowd..

_____

_____

Getting Started

❷ In your homework, you were asked to read about Joseph and how he forgave his brothers for selling him into slavery. Ultimately, Joseph concluded that God had used the situation to enable Joseph to provide for his family during the seven years of famine. Please share a story of a difficult or hurtful situation that became something good in the end.

_____

_____

_____

_____

_____

Jesus Knows Your Pain --- Everyone is Against Me!

Shame can arise from the way that an entire group of people chooses to treat a person. The group might be a circle of friends, a neighborhood, a group of co-workers, the town or community or the entire country. It can arise through shaming tactics often found in the form of bullying, mobbing, shunning, or discrimination. Again, volunteers are encouraged to read this piece aloud.

Tracy's Story

They thought it was funny, but I didn't. Sure, I suppose that it was harmless fun, but I was so embarrassed. I hated to go out on the manufacturing floor. It was all men that worked there. Their manager was also a man. It was a summer job for me. I was an expeditor. Basically, I had to take the blueprints or job orders or tools to the guys working on the manufacturing floor, confirm that they had all of the parts needed for the job and ensure that the jobs were being completed in the order needed, without unnecessary delays.

Well, the guys all had squirt guns at their work stations. When I wasn't looking, they would squirt me with water on the back of my clothes. Sometimes they'd try to get the front of my clothes. Of course, they aimed for my most private areas. Their manager just thought it was funny. "Oh, boys will be boys," he'd respond to my complaints. "Just ignore it." I tried to ignore it; but I hated it. It was humiliating. It was so personally invasive for me, that I found myself suddenly feeling as though my clothing was wet even when I was shopping or otherwise away from work. I was so relieved when the summer ended and I could quit that job. —Tracy

Kara's Story

We just moved to a new town. I was starting in the second grade. I was so excited. I loved school, until I got to the new school. Reading class was very different than in my old school. The reading books were so much harder. I could read a little; but not what they expected me to do at this school. I hated it when the teacher called on me to read out loud. I couldn't do it and I could just feel everyone staring at me. When we had tests that involved reading or vocabulary or spelling, I often got "D's" and "F's." The teacher would write the grade on my paper in big, red letters. Everyone noticed. I felt so dumb. The kids were mean about it. I could hear their whispers. Every night, my mom tried to help me do my school work; but it took so long because I was crying most of the time. "I can't do it!" I'd sob. "I'm stupid." —Kara

Alyson's Story

I grew up in a home of an angry alcoholic mother and an angry violent father. My mom began drinking everyday at 4:00 p.m., and then she and one of my brothers spent the rest of the night cruelly verbally attacking me. When my father got home from work, he joined in. Throughout my life, whether drunk or sober, angry or in perfect calm, my parents told me under no uncertain terms that I was inadequate, unlovable, and unworthy. They left nothing to the imagination! This occurred as long as I remember.

I have no positive memories, only memories of being ridiculed and verbally and physically attacked. I was miserable as far back as I remember. I counted the days until I could get out of that environment; I thought the time would never pass quickly enough. Despite being told I was lazy, stupid, a slut, and an overall miserable being not deserving of anything, I patiently and methodically made plans for college and a career (against the vociferous objections of my parents) so I could become self-sufficient and escape my prison.

In time my four younger brothers, all of whom watched on as I was the recipient of my parents' wrath, learned to treat me in the same manner. Now they continue the tradition. Ultimately, one of their wives kicked me out of the family.

> **Promises to Keep**
>
> A poor man is shunned by all his relatives—how much more do his friends avoid him! Though he pursues them with pleading, they are nowhere to be found.
> Proverbs 19:7

Though I have grieved for many years, I knew in my heart that God removed me from that very sick situation to protect my own family. God promised me that the family curse would stop with me. He promised me complete deliverance and freedom from their curse. I have relied on that promise throughout my adult life. God also brought many awesome Christians into my life as models to follow. God has brought many people from many walks of life to cross my path with words of esteem and encouragement. —Alyson

Shaming by bullying may include belittling, constant fault-finding, nit-picking, or humiliating a person over and over again. It happens among school kids, within families, and within communities. Once started, often by a single person, it can spread like a disease to the entire social circle. The victims are often treated so badly, for so long, they don't even recognize when a similar pattern is starting in a new social circle until it is too late. The victims often develop a sense of worthlessness or unacceptability.

Shaming by mobbing is basically bullying in the work place. Mobbing occurs when co-workers, subordinates or superiors "gang up" on a person to force him or her out of the workplace through "rumor, innuendo, intimidation, humiliation, discrediting, and isolation."[1] Mobbing may involve threatening, intimidating or hostile acts directed at a co-worker; generally abrasive behavior; using obscene, abusive or threatening language or gestures; discrediting a co-worker; slander; withholding information vital to the co-worker's job performance; acts of physical or emotional isolation; prohibiting due process; and retribution for pursuing due process.[2]

Shaming by shunning is a means to instill conformance to the society's expectations by deliberately avoiding someone, or preventing him or her to be a part of the group. The Scarlet Letter by Nathaniel Hawthorne is a perfect example of a shunning tactic. In that story, a young woman named Hester Prynne, was required to wear a scarlet letter "A" sewn onto her clothing and to stand on a scaffold in the public square as punishment for her act of adultery. She was shamed by the entire community. She ultimately moved to the outskirts of the community where she lived a life of isolation, supporting her daughter and herself as a seamstress.

Discrimination can create feelings of shame in its victims. Just consider the days of the Jim Crow laws (which were in force in the United States between 1876 and 1964, primarily in the southern States), which imposed racial segregation in all public facilities. Shame often develops as the result of frequent, repeated, negative treatment directed at a person because of his or her differentiating features from the majority of the group, community, or in this case, a significant portion of the nation.

❸ Please share other examples of shame that may have been imposed upon a person by the actions of a larger group of people.

_____

_____

_____

_____

_____

❹ Why do you think that bullying, mobbing, or discrimination create feelings of shame, particularly when the person has done nothing wrong?

_____

_____

_____

_____

_____

5 What other feelings might a person have when bullied, mobbed or otherwise discriminated against?

_____

_____

_____

_____

_____

6 It has been said that one cannot change the way others treat him; but one can change the way he responds to the mistreatment. With that concept in mind, what suggestions would you give a person who is being bullied by his or her family, peers or workgroup?

_____

_____

_____

_____

_____

> **Promises to Keep**
>
> We who are strong ought to bear with the failings of the weak and not to please ourselves. Each of us should please his neighbor for his good, to build him up. For even Christ did not please himself but, as it is written: "The insults of those who insult you have fallen on me."
>
> Romans 15:1-3

Bible Study

Sometimes, as in The Scarlet Letter, the person who is being shamed by the community did something that was deemed inappropriate or sinful by the community. Please read the following Bible story about an adulterous woman. John 8:1-11:

But Jesus went to the Mount of Olives. At dawn he appeared again in the temple courts, where all the people gathered around him, and he sat down to teach them. The teachers of the law and the Pharisees brought in a woman caught in adultery. They made her stand before the group and said to Jesus, "Teacher, this woman was caught in the act of adultery. In the Law Moses commanded us to stone such women. Now what do you say?" They were using this question as a trap, in order to have a basis for accusing him.

But Jesus bent down and started to write on the ground with his finger. When they kept on questioning him, he straightened up and said to them, "If any one of you is without sin, let him be the first to throw a stone at her." Again he stooped down and wrote on the ground.

At this, those who heard began to go away one at a time, the older ones first, until only Jesus was left, with the woman still standing there. Jesus straightened up and asked her, "Woman, where are they? Has no one condemned you?"

"No one, sir," she said.

"Then neither do I condemn you," Jesus declared. "Go now and leave your life of sin."

7 Worse than being shunned, this woman was facing the death penalty. The leaders of the community had turned against her and they chose to use her to test Jesus. Before Jesus spoke, what did he do?

_____

_____

_____

_____

_____

8 We don't know what Jesus was writing in the sand; however, sometimes silence can have a positive impact on the crowd. If you were in the crowd at that time, what might you be thinking during this period of silence?

_____

_____

_____

_____

_____

9 What might we learn from Jesus through his initial silence in this situation?

_____

_____

_____

_____

_____

10 Jesus did not change the Law of Moses in his answer. However, how did Jesus get the crowd to choose not to stone the woman?

_____

_____

_____

_____

_____

11 No one was able to claim being without sin in this story. In our communities today, what does this tell us about those that belittle, bully or shame a person for differences or faults?

_____

_____

_____

_____

_____

12 What did Jesus tell the woman, after the crowd left?

_____

_____

_____

_____

_____

⓭ Discuss why the instruction given by Jesus to the woman is an important message for each of us.

_____

_____

_____

_____

_____

Often, bad things happen to us, or we are falsely accused of wrongdoing. The story of Job is an example of a man that was righteous, but faced total financial, familial and physical destruction (just short of death) at the hand of Satan. Instead of helping him, the community abandoned him, as described by Job himself, in Job 19:13-20. Try to imagine being in Job's shoes as you read this Bible passage.

> *"He has alienated my brothers from me;*
> *my acquaintances are completely estranged from me.*
> *My kinsmen have gone away;*
> *my friends have forgotten me.*
> *My guests and my maidservants count me a stranger;*
> *they look upon me as an alien.*
> *I summon my servant, but he does not answer,*
> *though I beg him with my own mouth.*
> *My breath is offensive to my wife;*
> *I am loathsome to my own brothers.*
> *Even the little boys scorn me;*
> *when I appear, they ridicule me.*
> *All my intimate friends detest me;*
> *those I love have turned against me.*
> *I am nothing but skin and bones;*
> *I have escaped with only the skin of my teeth."*

Some of us may have been treated similarly by our families or our communities. When things are going badly, instead of helping, the entire community seems to add to the problem. Job's friends told him to repent of his sins, because it was clear that his misfortune was God's punishment. However, Job would not allow the opinions of his friends to convince him to accept undeserved blame or shame. Please read Job's words in reply to his friends' accusations, as written in Job 27:5-6, printed below.

I will never admit you are in the right;
till I die, I will not deny my integrity.
I will maintain my righteousness and never let go of it;
my conscience will not reproach me as long as I live.

Ultimately, Job questioned God about Job's lot in life, demanding that God show him why God has allowed everything to be taken from him. God sternly reminded Job that he is all powerful and that no man can understand his ways. Job knew this to be true and he humbled himself before the Lord. Then, God made Job prosperous again.

14 Like Job, we may face loss or we may be mistreated by others in our community, based on no wrongdoing of our own. Looking at Job's response to his accusers and then to God, what advice would you give a friend that is facing unjust treatment from a group?

_____

_____

_____

_____

_____

> **Promises to Keep**
> Bless those who persecute you; bless and do not curse.
> Romans 12:14

Please read the following Bible passages about Jesus' life.
Isaiah 53:3:

He was despised and rejected by men, a man of sorrows, and familiar with suffering. Like one from whom men hide their faces he was despised, and we esteemed him not.

Mark 6:1-4:

Jesus left there and went to his hometown, accompanied by his disciples. When the Sabbath came, he began to teach in the synagogue, and many who heard him were amazed. "Where did this man get these things?" they asked. "What's this wisdom that has been given him, that he even does miracles! Isn't this the carpenter? Isn't this Mary's son and the brother of James, Joseph, Judas and Simon? Aren't his sisters here with us?" And they took offense at him. Jesus said to them, "Only in his hometown, among his relatives and in his own house is a prophet without honor."

Matthew 27:27-30:

Then the governor's soldiers took Jesus into the Praetorium and gathered the whole company of soldiers around him. They stripped him and put a scarlet robe on him, and then twisted together a crown of thorns and set it on his head. They put a staff in his right hand and knelt in front of him and mocked him. "Hail, king of the Jews!" they said. They spit on him, and took the staff and struck him on the head again and again. After they had mocked him, they took off the robe and put his own clothes on him. Then they led him away to crucify him.

Isaiah 53:9:

*He was assigned a grave with the wicked,
and with the rich in his death,
though he had done no violence,
nor was any deceit in his mouth.*

15 Compare Jesus' experiences with those of someone that is shamed by his or her group or community today through bullying, mobbing, or discriminations.

_____
_____
_____
_____
_____

16 How do we know that God will understand how we feel when we are being unjustly treated by those around us?

_____
_____
_____
_____
_____

> **Promises to Keep**
>
> Great is our Lord and mighty in power; his understanding has no limit. The Lord sustains the humble but casts the wicked to the ground.
>
> Psalm 147:5-6

Reflection & Encouragement

"Whenever evil befalls us, we ought to ask ourselves, after the first suffering, how we can turn it into good. So shall we take occasion, from one bitter root, to raise perhaps many flowers."

Leigh Hunt

Closing Prayer

Lord Jesus, our Savior, we humble ourselves before you, knowing that you faced the ultimate injustice through crucifixion, all out of love for us. You know the afflictions that we have faced, some of which have been deserved and some of which cannot be justified. In the words of David, as is written in Psalm 109, we pray.

But you, O Sovereign Lord,
deal well with me for your name's sake,
out of the goodness of your love, deliver me.
For I am poor and needy,
and my heart is wounded within me.
I am the object of scorn to my accusers;
when they see me, they shake their heads.
…Help me, O Lord my God;
save me in accordance with your love.
Let them know that it is your hand,
that you O Lord, have done it.
They may curse, but you will bless;
when they attack they will be put to shame,
but your servant will rejoice.

We trust in your love for us. We rely on your strength and your wisdom and your understanding. Amen.

Week 8 Memory Verse

With my mouth I will greatly extol the Lord;
in the great throng I will praise him.
For he stands at the right hand of the needy one,
to save his life from those who condemn him.

Psalm 109:30-31

Homework

❶ Are you aware of any forms of bullying, mobbing, shunning or discrimination in any of your social or work or church communities? List them in your journal.

❷ Pray that God will soften your heart to these circumstances and teach you how to stop any unjust treatment. Ask for the courage to take the action needed to stop any unjust treatment. Write this prayer in your journal.

❸ Are you the victim of any community-based bullying, either at work or in your social circles or within your church? Pray that God will open your eyes, enabling you to truly recognize whether you have done anything that needs correction. Pray that he gives you the strength to stand up to any unjust treatment with integrity. If you have blamed God for this unjust treatment by others, humble yourself and seek his forgiveness. Add this prayer to your journal.

❹ Read Week 9 in preparation for the next meeting.

Notes

1. "Home page." Mobbing - USA: Emotional Abuse in the American Workplace. June 30, 2006. September 16, 2006. <http://www.mobbing-usa.com/index.html>.

2. 2. "State of Oregon, Department of Environmental Quality ANTI-MOBBING POLICY no. 50.110." Mobbing - USA: Emotional Abuse in the American Workplace. June 30, 2006. September 16, 2006. <http://www.mobbing-usa.com/R_legal.html>.

Week 9

I Didn't Do It

it's not my shame

For they loved praise from men more than praise from God.
John 12:43

Opening Prayer

Almighty God, we come to you again as a group that needs you and your loving care. Help us to understand what issues cause us to feel pain in our hearts. Help us to know where our responsibility starts and where it ends. Teach us to accept responsibility when it is our duty to do so. At the same time, enable us to let go of the things that burden our hearts, for which we have no control. In those cases, we give such burdens to you, Lord, trusting in your everlasting love and grace. Amen.

Meeting & Greeting

We are now starting our ninth week in this Grapple with Guilt, Shed the Shame covenant group. We have learned about the many sources of shame, whether it is based on our own unresolved guilt or on the actions of others. Yet in this week, we will learn about one more source of shame.

❶ To begin, describe something that is in your house that you would bring to "Show and Tell" if you were in elementary school today. Explain why you would pick this particular item for "Show and Tell."

_____

_____

_____

Getting Started

❷ In Week 8, we looked at shame that is felt as the result of various forms of bullying, including shunning, mobbing and discrimination. Gossip can also result in feelings of shame. The author feared the community gossip and the resultant shame it would bring when she discovered that she was pregnant. Discuss the many ways that gossip can hurt a person.

❸ Discuss ways to stop gossip first as one hearing the gossip, then as one that is the subject of the gossip.

I Didn't Do It—It's Not My Shame

Sometimes, out of embarrassment or perhaps love, we take on the shame that actually belongs to someone else. For example, I can't help but feel badly for the parents of a criminal. It must cause them pain to have their adult child's picture plastered in the papers, knowing that everyone has read or is talking about the criminal act that he or she committed. Yet, they are not responsible for their adult child's actions. The shame does not belong to them; it belongs to their son or daughter. Please read the following stories aloud.

Jodi's Story

I recall a situation that must have been very difficult for a friend of mine. It happened when I was in junior high school. I had been spending the hours after school with my friend, and I was going to spend the night at her house. At dinner time, she made dinner for us as her parents weren't home. They were at the local tavern. They were always at the local tavern, every day it seemed. When she wanted permission to do something with me, we would simply go there to find her parents. That particular evening, we had a very good time, staying up late, watching movies on the television, and generally talking and giggling as any young girls are inclined to do. Shortly after midnight, my friend made it clear that we should go to bed, as it would not be good to still be up when her parents got home. Not too long after we went to bed, her parents came home. We could hear them arguing. There was a lot of noise, sounding like someone had fallen over or into something. It sounded like they were having a fight. It was quite obvious, just from the voices and noises, that her parents were drunk. My friend urgently whispered, "No matter what happens, pretend to be asleep." Shortly after that, the house got quiet again. I assumed her parents went to bed. My friend never invited me to her house again. She was likely ashamed of what had happened. —Jodi

Emma's Story

I almost didn't marry him; but he promised that he wouldn' t drink anymore, at least not that much. He said he was just having fun. After we were married, we moved about four hours away by car. At first, he kept his promises; but in time he went back to his old self. He was always the life of the party. Everybody loved him. But he never seemed to know when to quit drinking. He'd frequently go out for "just one" after work with the guys. He wouldn't call. He'd come home at all hours of the night. I was so angry and hurt. How could he do that to me? I'd cry to myself.

We lived in a small town. I assumed everyone knew about his drinking. I'd get so embarrassed whenever someone would tell me that they saw him out the night before. They never said anything bad about him. If fact, they always noted the good time they all had. I wondered if they could tell when he had too much to drink. I could tell as soon as he'd walk in the door. I could see it in his eyes. I could hear it in his voice.

It seemed that he'd be fine for a long time; and then it was like someone pulled the switch, and he'd be drunk.

After a few years, we moved back to my home town, where my mom and dad still lived. I was so worried that they would discover how much he drank. I couldn't tell them. I never talked about it to anyone. But this town was so small, I was sure that they would find out. I didn't want them to know. What would they think of him, or me, or my marriage?

He kept on with his old habits: going out after work, with who knows who; drinking until all hours; and never calling. Sometimes I'd wait up, and other times I'd try to sleep and ignore him when he got home. I was so tired of his excuses. I was so ashamed of his drinking and carousing. No one in town ever said anything negative about him, but I always worried about what they thought.

Ultimately, as the kids got older, I'd try to hide his drinking from them by lying. He has a meeting. He's bowling with the guys. He had to stay late tonight to get some paperwork done. I made so many excuses for him.

How much longer, God, do I have to put up with this? I'd silently pray. —Emma

Tim's Story

I was six years old when my mom came into my room and told me that Daddy wasn't going to live with us anymore. She told me that they were going to get a divorce, and that then they would not be married any more. "Does that mean that I won't have a daddy anymore?" I asked? "No, you will always have your daddy. He loves you. It's just that he and I don't love each other," Mommy replied. Then she left the room. When did he quit loving her? I wondered. Was it when they had a fight? He hit her sometimes. He hit me sometimes too. Then they would really get in a fight. Maybe it was my fault.

At first, Daddy would take me to his new house. I'd get to see him on weekends. But sometimes I'd be ready to go to his house, waiting by the window, but he wouldn't show up. After some months, I quit waiting because he quit coming. He didn't love me anymore, I thought to myself. He didn't want to be with me, that's why he divorced Mom. It was my fault. I was always bad, and they always fought about me. I messed up the house; I wouldn't eat my dinner; and I'd yell back at my dad. I should have been nicer to him. I thought nobody loved me and that nobody would ever want to love me. - Tim

4 In each of the examples above, each person accepted shame that really belonged to someone else. Discuss in each case who was the one that should have felt shame based on his or her actions..

_____
_____
_____
_____
_____

5 List other examples in which a person might carry the shame that actually belongs to another person.

_____
_____
_____
_____
_____

6 Why do you think that people accept shame upon themselves when someone else is really at fault? Try to list at least 5 reasons.

_____
_____
_____
_____
_____

> **Promises to Keep**
>
> "Therefore, O house of Israel, I will judge you, each one according to his ways," declares the Sovereign Lord. Repent! Turn away from all your offenses; then sin will not be your downfall.
>
> Ezekiel 18:30

Bible Study

Often, when we adopt others' shame, it is because we care deeply for them. Perhaps they are our sons, daughters, or spouses. We often feel the shame that we think they should feel. We also feel shame that we believe is reflected on us, on perhaps our parenting skills or our choices in a spouse or friends. Please read the following passages from Ezekiel 18:5, 9-18, 20.

"Suppose there is a righteous man
who does what is just and right.
…He follows my decrees
and faithfully keeps my laws.
That man is righteous;
he will surely live,
declares the Sovereign Lord.
"Suppose he has a violent son, who sheds blood or does any of these other things (though the father has done none of them):
"He eats at the mountain shrines.
He defiles his neighbor's wife.
He oppresses the poor and needy.
He commits robbery.
He does not return what he took in pledge.
He looks to the idols.
He does detestable things.
He lends at usury and takes excessive interest.
Will such a man live? He will not! Because he has done all these detestable things, he will surely be put to death and his blood will be on his own head.
"But suppose this son has a son who sees all the sins his father commits, and though he sees them, he does not do such things:
"He does not eat at the mountain shrines
or look to the idols of the house of Israel.
He does not defile his neighbor's wife.
He does not oppress anyone
or require a pledge for a loan.
He does not commit robbery
but gives his food to the hungry
and provides clothing for the naked.
He withholds his hand from sin
and takes no usury or excessive interest.
He keeps my laws and follows my decrees.
He will not die for his father's sin; he will surely live. But his father will die for his own sin, because he practiced extor-

tion, robbed his brother and did what was wrong among his people.

…The soul who sins is the one who will die. The son will not share the guilt of the father, nor will the father share the guilt of the son. The righteousness of the righteous man will be credited to him, and the wickedness of the wicked will be charged against him."

7 Here we read about the behavior of a father, his son and his grandson. The son was leading a sinful life. According to these passages, who will God hold responsible for the sins of the son?

_____

_____

_____

_____

_____

8 Do you think that the father or the grandson would feel any shame over what the son is doing? Why or why not?

_____

_____

_____

_____

_____

9 Do you think that God wants us to feel shame over the sinful behavior of those that we love? Discuss your reasoning.

_____

_____

_____

_____

_____

> **Promises to Keep**
>
> So then, each of us will give an account of himself to God.
>
> Romans 14:12

Please read the following story about Noah, and the actions of his sons after Noah put himself in a position of shame. Genesis 9:18-27:

"Noah, a man of the soil, proceeded to plant a vineyard. When he drank some of its wine, he became drunk and lay uncovered inside his tent. Ham, the father of Canaan, saw his father's nakedness and told his two brothers outside. But Shem and Japheth took a garment and laid it across their shoulders; then they walked in backward and covered their father's nakedness. Their faces were turned the other way so that they would not see their father's nakedness.

When Noah awoke from his wine and found out what his youngest son had done to him, he said, "Cursed be Canaan! The lowest of slaves will he be to his brothers."

He also said, "Blessed be the Lord, the God of Shem! May Canaan be the slave of Shem. May God extend the territory of Japheth, may Japheth live in the tents of Shem, and may Canaan be his slave."

❿ Describe the difference between the way that Ham treated his father and the way that the other sons treated their father.

_____

_____

_____

_____

_____

⓫ Japheth and Shem seemed to want to protect their father from shame. Do you think that by trying to provide this protection, they were condoning his behavior? Discuss.

_____

_____

12 Noah blessed his sons that helped him in a respectful manner. What can we learn from this story regarding how to treat our loved ones when they do something shameful?

_____

_____

_____

_____

_____

> **Promises to Keep**
>
> Above all, love each other deeply, because love covers over a multitude of sins.
> 1 Peter 4:8

We can't agree with one's behavior when we know that the behavior is wrong. Sometimes the behavior causes us to feel shame. Admonishment, suggestions or other well-intended advice is not always well-received. Please read the following passages on how one might resolve such a situation.

Galatians 6:2:
> *Carry each other's burdens, and in this way you will fulfill the law of Christ.*

1 Thessalonians 5:14-15:
> *And we urge you, brothers, warn those who are idle, encourage the timid, help the weak, be patient with everyone. Make sure that nobody pays back wrong for wrong, but always try to be kind to each other and to everyone else.*

Jesus, in Matthew 18:15-17:
> *"If your brother sins against you, go and show him his fault, just between the two of you. If he listens to you, you have won your brother over. But if he will not listen, take one or two others along, so that every matter may be established by the testimony of two or three witnesses. If he refuses to listen to them, tell it to the church; and if he refuses*

to listen even to the church, treat him as you would a pagan or a tax collector."

1 Thessalonians 5:16-18:

Be joyful always; pray continually; give thanks in all circumstances, for this is God's will for you in Christ Jesus.

2 Corinthians 3:5:

It is not that we think we can do anything of lasting value by ourselves. Our only power and success come from God.

❸ Based on the above passages, is it best to try to correct someone's behavior? How? Include in your discussion the ways that we might involve God in the process.

_____
_____
_____
_____
_____

❹ The verse from Galatians, chapter 6, states that we are to carry each other's burdens. This verse does not mean that we are to carry their shame. Discuss what it likely means instead.

_____
_____
_____
_____
_____

❺ Identify ways that you might help someone you love move away from his or her shameful behaviors.

_____
_____
_____
_____
_____

Week 9: I Didn't Do It / 147

16 There is a formal process often used by counselors called "intervention." It typically involves a number of people that care for the individual that is having trouble with addiction or another problem. They first prepare for a meeting with the person. Then they approach the person and talk to him or her in a clear but respectful manner. The goal is to make an impact on the person, and get him or her to listen and ultimately accept help. Which one of the above Bible passages describes a process similar to "intervention"?

_____

_____

_____

_____

_____

Sometimes, the person will not change his or her behavior. Please read the following passages for ideas on ways to shed shame that we have adopted as a result of the sinful behavior of another person.

Psalm 62:7-8:
> *My salvation and my honor depend on God,*
> *he is my mighty rock, my refuge.*
> *Trust in him at all times, O people;*
> *pour out your hearts to him, for God is our refuge.*

1 Peter 5:6-7:
> *Humble yourselves, therefore, under God's mighty hand, that he may lift you up in due time. Cast all your anxiety on him because he cares for you.*

Philippians 4:4-7:
> *Rejoice in the Lord always, I will say it again: Rejoice! Let your gentleness be evident to all. The Lord is near. Do not be anxious about anything, but in everything, by prayer and petition, with thanksgiving, present your requests to God. And the peace of God, which transcends all understanding, will guard your hearts and your minds in Christ Jesus.*

Isaiah 50:7:
> *Because the Sovereign Lord helps me,*
> *I will not be disgraced.*
> *Therefore have I set my face like flint,*
> *and I know I will not be put to shame*

17 No matter how hard we try to help some people, sometimes we cannot get them to change their behaviors. Looking at each passage above, make a list of the things we can do to shed the shame that we have adopted based on the actions of another.

_____

_____

_____

_____

_____

> **Promises to Keep**
>
> Therefore, there is now no condemnation for those who are in Christ Jesus, because through Christ Jesus the law of the Spirit of life set me free from the law of sin and death.
>
> Romans 8:1

Reflection & Encouragement

In Jules Verne's novel The Mysterious Island he tells of five men who escape a Civil War prison camp by hijacking a hot-air balloon.

As they rise into the air, they realize the wind is carrying them over the ocean. With the surface of the ocean drawing closer, the men decide they must cast some of the weight overboard. Shoes, overcoats, and weapons are reluctantly discarded, and the uncomfortable aviators feel their balloon rise.

However, it isn't long before they find themselves dangerously close to the waves again, so they toss their food overboard. Unfortunately, this too, is only a temporary solution and the craft again threatens to lower the men into the sea. They finally tie the ropes that hold the passenger car and sit on them so they can cut away the basket beneath them. As they do this, the balloon rises again.

Not a minute too soon, they spot land. They are alive because they were able to discern the difference between what was really needed and what was not. The "necessities" they once thought they couldn't live without were the very

weights that almost cost them their lives.
(Excerpted from *Coffee Break with God: Honor Books*.)

Is the shame that you have adopted as the result of another person's actions a necessity in your life? How long will you allow this shame to cost you your life or your peace? Isn't it time to throw it overboard?

Closing Prayer

Father, God. Thank you for showing us that we do not need to carry the burden of shame that we so often feel when those that are close to us make disappointing, dangerous or sinful choices. We thank you for not holding us responsible for the failings of others. However, we know that we should help them in their time of need, showing them how to return to the path that you want them to take. Help us to love them; and show us how and when to give them help. In all cases, we know that you are in control, and that we must give our anxiety and shame to you. Thank you for taking this burden from our shoulders. The weight is too great for us to carry. Thank you for your peace. Amen.

Week 9 Memory Verse

Peace I leave with you; my peace I give you.

Jesus, John 14:27

Homework

❶ Do you have someone in your life whose behaviors have caused you to feel shame? Write about this situation in your journal, and pray that God will enable to you treat this person with love and respect, and to help him or her find a path that honors God.

❷ Consider whether counseling or intervention is possibly needed. Consult with your pastoral leadership at your church or with a Christian counselor about your best options.

❸ In your journal, make a list of your feelings when you are faced with shame that is caused by someone else's behavior. Pray over this list, asking Jesus to relieve you of this burden.

❹ Please read through Week 10 in preparation for the next discussion.

Week 10

I Shed the Shame

with God is joy

> *May the God of hope fill you with all joy and peace as you trust in him, so that you may overflow with hope by the power of the Holy Spirit.*
>
> Romans 15:13

Opening Prayer

Dear Holy Father, thank you for bringing us together each week to study the impact of shame on our lives. Thank you for giving us the wisdom to discern when the guilt or shame is the result of something we have done or something we have failed to do, and when the shame simply is not our responsibility. Help us to let go of the shame that does not belong to us, in ways that are helpful to those around us; and help us to continually reflect your love toward others. We pray in Jesus' name. Amen.

Meeting & Greeting

Welcome to our final week for the Grapple with Guilt, Shed the Shame covenant group.

❶ Please tell us about one of your favorite things to do when you want to relax, or "get away from it all."

_____

_____

_____

_____

Getting Started

❷ In your homework, you were asked to make a list of what shame feels like for you. What are some of the feelings that you put on the list.

_____

_____

_____

_____

❸ Shedding shame is not as easy as simply throwing a list of feelings in the trash. However, through faith and prayer, Christ will take these burdens from you. Did anyone feel a sense of relief when you gave your list of feelings to Christ through prayer? Please share your experience, if you are willing.

_____

_____

_____

_____

I Shed the Shame! With God is Joy

In this section, we will read about a woman (Ginny) whose shame-filled story is heartbreaking, intense, and occasionally shocking; yet through Christ, today she has peace in her heart. Her story is one that is ultimately filled with his goodness. It shows that God performs miracles through his love today, and always. As you read this final story, you will wonder how this loving woman found peace; then you will realize that peace in this case (as in many cases) is only possible through God, through the saving grace of our Lord, Jesus Christ. Hearing the peace in Ginny's voice as she told this story, reminds me that nothing is impossible with God, even in our darkest moments of life. Please read this final story as a group.

Ginny's Story

He was a big man, very tall, and very scary. He ruled the house with an iron fist, and I don't mean through strength based on inner resolve. He ruled the house literally with his fist, his belt, and his general ability to use brute force. He had guns in the house. They were loaded. I had no doubt that if he was pushed far enough, he would use one of them in a fit of rage.

Four o'clock in the afternoon was the worst. That was the time that he would come home from work. Every day was the same. He'd ask our mother how her day had gone. If there was anything wrong with her day, it was our fault. Our fault! There were five of us. I had an older sister, two younger brothers and one younger sister. She was the princess. It looked to my other sister and me that she was his favorite. She never had to endure quite the same abuse that the rest of us endured.

At four o'clock, no matter what we were doing, we learned quickly to go to our rooms and hide quietly, hoping our mother would say only good things about her day. It took so little to send him into a rage, a rage that could only be resolved through the heartless beating of at least one of us. Sometimes he'd beat my mother, sometimes me, sometimes my older sister, and sometimes my brothers.

The beatings were horrific, hideous and demeaning. There are no words to describe the shame that I felt in my heart. Imagine a young teenage girl, under the forceful hand of her father, being required to strip down to her skin so he could whip her mercilessly. He'd use whatever whipping device was most convenient. Usually it was his belt. At the same time, he would touch me. The pain was excruciating. The humiliation was unbearable. The physical and emotional results were unspeakable.

The beatings weren't the only issue. There was the touching. As long as I remember, he fondled me. I think I was four years old when it started. Even at that age, I knew that it wasn't right. I thought I was the only one. Then, once when I was fourteen years old, I caught him watching my older sister taking a bath. I caught him! It stunned me. We were such a private family. Everything was shrouded in secrecy. We talked to no one, not relatives, not friends, not even to each other. It wasn't until we were adults that my older sister and I finally talked about our experiences at home. We then learned that he sexually abused both of us. But he never touched his princess. I didn't understand it.

Abuse messes with your head. It stripped my soul bare until I was nothing. I always wondered what was wrong with me. I couldn't figure out why I could never measure up. I felt filthy. I believed that I was dirty. I had tremendous guilt. I was socially backward. The other kids at school were cruel to me. Every day was a struggle for me to just stay alive. I wanted to be accepted and loved. What does a young girl do with all of that unhealthy, sexual awakening? I went to any boy that looked at me. I pursued relationships, wanting to be loved. I discovered paths of promiscuity. Finally, when I was old enough, I moved out of the house, and directly into an abusive marriage. I stayed in that marriage for ten years. I thought that was all that I was worth.

During these horrific years, my grandmother would talk about her faith, but I couldn't and wouldn't trust God. I hated God for allowing these things to happen to me.

I was an adult before I learned the truth about my family relationships. This man that I thought was my father was actually my stepfather. He was my mother's second husband. While her first husband was in the service, she had an affair with another man and got pregnant. He was a player at that time, with no intention of helping her out of this complicated situation. So there she was with a daughter from her husband, and a baby on the way from an affair. When another man came into her life that was willing to marry her even though she was nearly nine months pregnant, she said yes. They moved to another state. I was born under this new husband's name. This wicked, sick man was not my natural father. Only the boys and the princess were his natural children.

It was such an incredible relief to me to know that I did not have that man's blood in my genes.

I began my search for my natural father.

I told one of my brothers about the whole story. I told him about searching for my natural father. I so wanted to share my story with him as I was so relieved about my new situation. I knew that my mother and my stepfather wouldn't approve, so I asked my brother not to say anything to them. Even though he promised silence, he told them anyway. Mom was furious. Perhaps, bringing to light her past mistakes brought her shame. That was the last that she or my stepfather ever spoke to me. I had lost my parents. They refused to talk with me, and they forbid my siblings to talk to me. None of them would talk to me. I found myself with no family. I tried for eight years to make contact, begging and humiliating myself, to no avail. As sick as that household was, it still pained me to be shunned by them. Who doesn't want their family to love them?

In time, my grandmother was able to make Jesus real for me, and she helped me build a relationship with him. I often turned to Psalm 27:10, which states, "Though my father and mother forsake me, the Lord will receive me." And receive me, he did.

Ultimately, God made it possible for me to find my natural father. He knew what I needed. He knew that I needed the love of a father. He knew and he provided. What some would call a coincidence, I call divine intervention.

I discovered that my mother's brother had been bowling in the same bowling league as my natural father for twenty years. Initially, when my natural father learned about me, he didn't want to meet me. But his wife called me anyway, and set up a meeting. That was over sixteen years ago. I finally met my natural father and we developed a wonderful relationship. I visited him and his wife for one week each year for the last sixteen years of my father's life. I had sixteen fabulous weeks with him, each week being a blessing from God. It was an amazing feeling to receive hugs from a man with no sexual overtones in them. God brought us together and blessed our lives with each other. My natural father and his wife became my new parents. His children became my new siblings. I had a new family.

When my grandmother died, I attended her funeral. It was the first time that I had seen my mother in over ten years. It was then that I fully came to realize that she and my stepfather were very, very, ill, either emotionally or mentally ill. They were the ones that were wrong, not I. I could now see their broken lives, lives that were controlled by Satan. Finally, I could look at them with sadness, maybe pity. I was able to give all of my pain to God, and I could look at them with forgiveness.

My life is now so rich and so wonderful. A big part of who I am is based in the fact that I was born out of pain. God saved me when he took me out of that sick, sick home. He blessed me with a new father, one who loved me the way a man is supposed to love his daughter. Even though he has since passed on, I still e-mail his wife daily. She is the woman that I love as my mother. God blessed me further with a new husband, a kind and understanding man. There were times over the years that something, maybe a name, a picture, or another reminder, would stir up anger and bitterness. But now I can say that there is peace, God's peace, a peace that only he can give. —Ginny

> **Promises to Keep**
>
> I am still confident of this:
> I will see the goodness of the Lord
> in the land of the living.
> Wait for the Lord;
> be strong and take heart
> and wait for the Lord.
>
> Psalm 27:13-14

4 Ginny mentions briefly that her grandmother made Christ "real" for her. Discuss what she might mean by the comment that Christ was now "real."

_____

_____

_____

_____

_____

5 Ginny doesn't mention what exactly her grandmother did to make Jesus "real" for her. List at least five things that a person could do to help another person discover that God is real. Think especially of someone that is angry with God or does not believe that a loving God exists in this hurting world.

_____

_____

_____

_____

_____

❻ Ginny's feelings moved from anger and bitterness to peace. Reviewing what we have learned or discussed in the prior weeks of this Bible study, list the things that may have occurred in Ginny's heart before she found peace.

_____

_____

_____

_____

_____

Bible Study

The life of the Apostle Paul, who was once known as Saul, was ultimately a life dedicated to serving Christ. He faced excruciating poverty, prison, and was even left for dead after being stoned. Yet he found joy in serving Jesus Christ. Let's together read about Paul's early life as Saul and his later conversion to be a follower of Christ, as told by Paul to King Agrippa in Acts 26:4-5, 9-18:

> *"The Jews all know the way I have lived ever since I was a child, from the beginning of my life in my own country, and also in Jerusalem. They have known me for a long time and can testify, if they are willing, that according to the strictest sect of our religion, I lived as a Pharisee."*

> *…"I too was convinced that I ought to do all that was possible to oppose the name of Jesus of Nazareth. And that is just what I did in Jerusalem. On the authority of the chief priests I put many of the saints in prison, and when they were put to death, I cast my vote against them. Many a time I went from one synagogue to another to have them punished, and I tried to force them to blaspheme. In my obsession against them, I even went to foreign cities to persecute them.*

> *"On one of these journeys I was going to Damascus with the authority and commission of the chief priests. About noon, O king, as I was on the road, I saw a light from heaven, brighter than the sun, blazing around me and my companions. We all fell to the ground, and I heard a voice saying to me in Aramaic, 'Saul, Saul, why do you persecute me? It is hard for you to kick against the goads.'*

> *"Then I asked, 'Who are you, Lord?'*

> *"'I am Jesus, whom you are persecuting,' the Lord replied.*

> *'Now get up and stand on your feet. I have appeared to you to appoint you as a servant and as a witness of what you*

have seen of me and what I will show you. I will rescue you from your own people and from the Gentiles. I am sending you to them to open their eyes and turn them from darkness to light, and from the power of Satan to God, so that they may receive forgiveness of sins and a place among those who are sanctified by faith in me."

7 Discuss what Paul (when living as Saul) did to those that believed in Jesus.

_____

_____

_____

_____

_____

8 Although Paul believed he was doing the right things, he was in fact a murderer. Yet, Jesus chose to use him and his past to bring others to faith in Christ. Discuss what this could mean about God's willingness to use you for his purposes, regardless of your past, your shame, or your guilty actions or inactions.

_____

_____

_____

_____

_____

> **Promises to Keep**
> The Lord works out everything for his own ends.
> Proverbs 16:3

After Paul's faith in Jesus was changed, he began preaching in the name of Jesus in attempt to make more believers in Christ. Such preaching was not always well received. Please read Paul's description of his life while preaching about Jesus, as described by him in his second letter to the Corinthians, chapter 11, verses 23-28.

Are they servants of Christ? (I am out of my mind to talk like this.) I am more. I have worked much harder, been in prison more frequently, been flogged more severely, and been exposed to death again and again. Five times I received from the Jews the forty lashes minus one. Three times I was beaten with rods, once I was stoned, three times I was shipwrecked, I spent a night and a day in the open sea, I have been constantly on the move. I have been in danger from rivers, in danger from bandits, in danger from my own countrymen, in danger from Gentiles; in danger in the city, in danger in the country, in danger at sea; and in danger from false brothers. I have labored and toiled and have often gone without sleep; I have known hunger and thirst and have often gone without food; I have been cold and naked. Besides everything else, I face daily the pressure of my concern for all the churches.

Based on the above, it is clear that even as a follower of Christ, doing God's will, our lives will not necessarily be pain free. In fact, for some of us, our circumstances may feel quite unbearable. However, Paul did not see this as a reason to abandon his faith. Instead, he found strength in his circumstances. Here is what he said to the Corinthians and to the Philippians.

2 Corinthians 12:7-10:

To keep me from becoming conceited because of these surpassingly great revelations, there was given me a thorn in my flesh, a messenger of Satan, to torment me. Three times I pleaded with the Lord to take it away from me. But he said to me, "My grace is sufficient for you, for my power is made perfect in weakness." Therefore I will boast all the more gladly about my weaknesses, so that Christ's power may rest on me. That is why, for Christ's sake, I delight in weaknesses, in insults, in hardships, in persecutions, in difficulties. For when I am weak, then I am strong.

Philippians 4:12-13:

I know what it is to be in need, and I know what it is to have plenty. I have learned the secret of being content in any and every situation, whether well fed or hungry, whether living in plenty or in want. I can do everything through him who gives me strength.

❾ Perhaps a prisoner of war understands the hardships that Paul has faced. Maybe a ransomed captive understands. I know there are many that have faced hardships similar to Ginny's story. Whatever the hardship, Paul concludes that he knows the secret to being content in any of these situations. What is that secret?

_____

_____

_____

_____

_____

Please read the following Bible passages as written by Paul.

Philippians 3:13-14:

Brothers, I do not consider myself yet to have taken hold of it. But one thing I do: Forgetting what is behind and straining toward what is ahead, I press on toward the goal to win the prize for which God has called me heavenward in Christ Jesus.

Philippians 4:4-9:

Rejoice in the Lord always. I will say it again: Rejoice! Let your gentleness be evident to all. The Lord is near. Do not be anxious about anything, but in everything, by prayer and petition, with thanksgiving, present your requests to God. And the peace of God, which transcends all understanding, will guard your hearts and your minds in Christ Jesus. Finally, brothers, whatever is true, whatever is noble, whatever is right, whatever is pure, whatever is lovely, whatever is admirable - if anything is excellent or praiseworthy - think about such things. Whatever you have learned or received or heard from me, or seen in me - put it into practice. And the God of peace will be with you.

Galatians 5:19-23:

The acts of the sinful nature are obvious: sexual immorality, impurity and debauchery; idolatry and witchcraft; hatred, discord, jealousy, fits of rage, selfish ambition, dissensions, factions and envy; drunkenness, orgies and the like. I warn you, as I did before, that those who live like this will not inherit the kingdom of God.

But the fruit of the Spirit is love, joy, peace, patience, kindness, goodness, faithfulness, gentleness and self-control. Against such things there is no law.

❿ What does Paul suggest we do to gain this strength in Christ, or to make him "real" in our lives?

_____

11 If Jesus is "real" in our lives, what can we expect to gain, according to Paul?

_____

_____

_____

_____

Jesus, himself has told us that he gives us peace in John 14:27, as printed below:

"Peace I leave with you; my peace I give you. I do not give to you as the world gives. Do not let your hearts be troubled and do not be afraid."

The author ultimately found peace in spite of her guilt over becoming pregnant and her shame over choosing abortion. While forgiveness does not remove the consequences of our sins, it will bring reconciliation with our Lord, even when forgiveness or reconciliation is not possible from or with the person that we have harmed.

Ginny faced years of shame as the result of the actions of her family. While reconciliation with her family is not likely, through Christ, she has found the ability to forgive her abusers. Then she was blessed by God with a new, loving family and through reconciliation with God. He has blessed her with joy and with peace. Reconciliation with our Lord brings us peace in all circumstances. Seek the Lord, give your burdens of guilt and shame to him, and bask in the security of his love. God will never leave you.

> **Promises to Keep**
>
> I pray also that the eyes of your heart may be enlightened in order that you may know the hope to which he has called you, the riches of his glorious inheritance in the saints, and his incomparably great power for us who believe.
>
> Ephesians 1:18-19

I pray that each of you discovers the peace and joy of living in Christ. If you have not yet accepted Jesus Christ as your Savior, I encourage you to confess your sins, and ask him to be your Savior, through the following prayer, or with words of your own choosing:

Dear God, I know that I have failed you in many ways, ways that have brought shame into my life or into the lives of others. I need you and I want you in my life. I thank you for sending your son, Jesus, to us, to pay the ultimate sacrifice for our sins through his death on the cross and his resurrection from the dead. I believe that through Jesus' sacrifice, I have been saved. Please forgive me for my many failures, failures made through my actions or my inactions. I want to live for you, with you, and in you. I ask that you live in me. I pray this in Jesus' holy name. Amen.

Reflection & Encouragement

"Peace is not the absence of conflict, but the presence of God no matter what the conflict."

Anonymous

Closing Prayer

Let's close this Bible study with the well-known prayer of St. Francis of Assisi, an Italian monk:

Lord, make me an instrument of Thy peace.
Where there is hatred, let me sow love.
Where there is injury, pardon. Where there is discord, unity.
Where there is doubt, faith. Where there is error, truth.
Where there is despair, hope. Where there is sadness, joy.
Where there is darkness, light.
For it is in giving, that we receive. It is in pardoning, that we are pardoned.
It is in dying, that we are born to eternal life.
Amen.

Week 10 Memory Verse

And we rejoice in the hope of the glory of God. Not only so, but we also rejoice in our sufferings, because

we know that suffering produces perseverance;
perseverance, character; and character, hope.

Romans 5:2b-3

Group Suggestion

- Before disbanding as a group, consider discussing whether your group members want to keep in touch, meet again, or otherwise continue the discussions that you all began through this Bible study.

Sources

References

Books

Beattie, Melody. *Codependent No More*. Center City, MN: Hazelden, 1992 by Hazelden Foundation.

Bolton, Martha. *Ouch: Encouragement for the Hurts of Life*. West Monroe, LA: Howard Publishing Co., Inc., 2006 by Martha Bolton.

Dollar, Dr. Creflo A. *Not Guilty: Experience God's Gift of Acceptance and Freedom*. Tulsa: Harrison House, 2002 by Dr. Creflo A. Dollar.

Douglas, J. D. New International Bible Dictionary. Zondervan; Revised ed.: 1999.

Evans, David G. *Healed Without Scars*. New Kensington, PA: Whitaker House, 2004 by David G. Evans.

Feider, Rev. Paul A. *Resting in the Heart: A Spirituality of Healing and Wholeness*. Eugene, OR: Wipf and Stock Publishers, 2001 by Paul A. Feider.

Green, Daniel and Mel Lawrenz. *Encountering Shame and Guilt: Resources for Strategic Pastoral Counseling*. Grand Rapids, MI: Baker Books, a Division of Baker Book House Co., 1994 by Daniel R. Green and Mel Lawrenz.

Green, Daniel and Mel Lawrenz. *Why Do I Feel Like Hiding? How to Overcome Shame and Guilt*. Grand Rapids, MI: Baker Books, a Division of Baker Book House Co., 1994 by Mel Lawrenz and Daniel Green.

Johnson, Hiram. *Tragic Redemption: Healing the Guilt and Shame*. Austin, TX: Langmarc Publishing, 2006 by Hiram Johnson.

MacDonald, Gordon. *Rebuilding Your Broken World*. Nashville, TN: Thomas Nelson Publishers, a division of Thomas Nelson, Inc., 1990 by Gordon MacDonald, Repackaged edition 2003.

McNish, Jill L., Ph.D. *Transforming Shame: A Pastoral Response*. Binghamton, NY: The Haworth Pastoral Press, an imprint of The Haworth Press, Inc., 2004 by the Haworth Press, Inc.

Middleton-Moz, Jane. *Shame & Guilt: The Masters of Disguise*. Deerfield Beach, FL: Health Communications, Inc., 1990 by Jane Middleton-Moz.

Potter-Efron, Ronald and Patricia Potter-Efron. *Letting Go of Shame: Understanding How Shame Affects Your Life*. Center City, MN: Hazelden®, 1989 by Robert T. Potter-Efron and Patricia S. Potter-Efron.

Smedes, Lewis B. *Shame and Grace: Healing the Shame We Don't Deserve.* New York, NY: HarperSanFrancisco and Zondervan Publishing House, Divisions of HarperCollins Publishers, 1993 by Lewis B. Smedes.

Wright, Alan D. *Shame Off You: Washing Away the Mud That Hides Our True Selves.* Sisters, OR: Multnomah® Publishers, Inc., 2005 by Alan D. Wright.

Online Resources

Green, Daniel, Ph.D. and Mel Lawrenz, Ph.D. "Coming Out of Hiding." 1996 by Christian Care Resources (CareRes@aol.com). New Life Resources, Inc. April 27, 2006. <http://www.newliferesourcesinc.com>.

Kelley, Doug. "Get Rid of Guilt and Shame! What I Do Is Not Necessarily Who I Am." Reprinted from The Game Rules for Life, June 2000, Empowered Recovery. June 12, 2006.
<http://www.empoweredrecovery.com/articles/uilit.htm>.

Miller, Marc, Ph.D. "Shame and Psychotherapy." March 19, 2006. Columbia Psychotherapy Associates. May 31, 2006.
<http://www.columbiapsych.com/shame_miller.html>.

Norton, Amy. "Verbally Abused Kids May Become Depressed Adults." Reuters Health. June 1, 2006. MedlinePlus. June 12, 2006.
http://www.nlm.nih.gov/medlineplus/news/fullstory_34311.html>.

Smallwood, Beverly, Ph.D. "Is Your Guilt Constructive…or Destructive?" Copyright unknown. May 31, 2006. <http://hodu.com/destructive.shtml>.

Tucker-Ladd, Clayton E. Psychological Self-Help. 1996-2000 by Clayton Tucker-Ladd & Mental Health Net. May 31, 2006.
<http://www.mentalhelp.net/psyhelp/>.

Scripture

Memory Verses

The following pages have the memory verses from each week/chapter. The pages have been formatted for easy removal. Cut out the memory verse for each particular week. Place copies of it in easy to notice locations throughout your home, office and car, enabling you to read it several times a day, and commit it to memory.

Week 1 Memory Verse

For the eyes of the Lord range throughout the earth to strengthen those whose hearts are fully committed to him. 2 Chronicles 16:9	For the eyes of the Lord range throughout the earth to strengthen those whose hearts are fully committed to him. 2 Chronicles 16:9
For the eyes of the Lord range throughout the earth to strengthen those whose hearts are fully committed to him. 2 Chronicles 16:9	For the eyes of the Lord range throughout the earth to strengthen those whose hearts are fully committed to him. 2 Chronicles 16:9
For the eyes of the Lord range throughout the earth to strengthen those whose hearts are fully committed to him. 2 Chronicles 16:9	For the eyes of the Lord range throughout the earth to strengthen those whose hearts are fully committed to him. 2 Chronicles 16:9

Week 2 Memory Verse

Yet to all who received him, to those who believed in his name, he gave the right to become children of God. John 1:12	Yet to all who received him, to those who believed in his name, he gave the right to become children of God. John 1:12
Yet to all who received him, to those who believed in his name, he gave the right to become children of God. John 1:12	Yet to all who received him, to those who believed in his name, he gave the right to become children of God. John 1:12
Yet to all who received him, to those who believed in his name, he gave the right to become children of God. John 1:12	Yet to all who received him, to those who believed in his name, he gave the right to become children of God. John 1:12

Week 3 Memory Verse

Let us draw near to God with a sincere heart in full assurance of faith, having our hearts sprinkled to cleanse us from a guilty conscience and having our bodies washed with pure water. Hebrews 10:22	Let us draw near to God with a sincere heart in full assurance of faith, having our hearts sprinkled to cleanse us from a guilty conscience and having our bodies washed with pure water. Hebrews 10:22
Let us draw near to God with a sincere heart in full assurance of faith, having our hearts sprinkled to cleanse us from a guilty conscience and having our bodies washed with pure water. Hebrews 10:22	Let us draw near to God with a sincere heart in full assurance of faith, having our hearts sprinkled to cleanse us from a guilty conscience and having our bodies washed with pure water. Hebrews 10:22
Let us draw near to God with a sincere heart in full assurance of faith, having our hearts sprinkled to cleanse us from a guilty conscience and having our bodies washed with pure water. Hebrews 10:22	Let us draw near to God with a sincere heart in full assurance of faith, having our hearts sprinkled to cleanse us from a guilty conscience and having our bodies washed with pure water. Hebrews 10:22

Week 4 Memory Verse

For all have sinned and fall short of the glory of God, and are justified freely by his grace through the redemption that came by Christ Jesus. Romans 3:23-24	For all have sinned and fall short of the glory of God, and are justified freely by his grace through the redemption that came by Christ Jesus. Romans 3:23-24
For all have sinned and fall short of the glory of God, and are justified freely by his grace through the redemption that came by Christ Jesus. Romans 3:23-24	For all have sinned and fall short of the glory of God, and are justified freely by his grace through the redemption that came by Christ Jesus. Romans 3:23-24
For all have sinned and fall short of the glory of God, and are justified freely by his grace through the redemption that came by Christ Jesus. Romans 3:23-24	For all have sinned and fall short of the glory of God, and are justified freely by his grace through the redemption that came by Christ Jesus. Romans 3:23-24

Week 5 Memory Verse

There is rejoicing in the presence of the angels of God over one sinner who repents. Luke 15:10	There is rejoicing in the presence of the angels of God over one sinner who repents. Luke 15:10
There is rejoicing in the presence of the angels of God over one sinner who repents. Luke 15:10	There is rejoicing in the presence of the angels of God over one sinner who repents. Luke 15:10
There is rejoicing in the presence of the angels of God over one sinner who repents. Luke 15:10	There is rejoicing in the presence of the angels of God over one sinner who repents. Luke 15:10

Week 6 Memory Verse

In him we have redemption through his blood, the forgiveness of sins, in accordance with the riches of God's grace. Ephesians 1:7	In him we have redemption through his blood, the forgiveness of sins, in accordance with the riches of God's grace. Ephesians 1:7
In him we have redemption through his blood, the forgiveness of sins, in accordance with the riches of God's grace. Ephesians 1:7	In him we have redemption through his blood, the forgiveness of sins, in accordance with the riches of God's grace. Ephesians 1:7
In him we have redemption through his blood, the forgiveness of sins, in accordance with the riches of God's grace. Ephesians 1:7	In him we have redemption through his blood, the forgiveness of sins, in accordance with the riches of God's grace. Ephesians 1:7

Week 7 Memory Verse

Don't let evil get the best of you, but conquer evil by doing good. Romans 12:21 (NLT)	Don't let evil get the best of you, but conquer evil by doing good. Romans 12:21 (NLT)
Don't let evil get the best of you, but conquer evil by doing good. Romans 12:21 (NLT)	Don't let evil get the best of you, but conquer evil by doing good. Romans 12:21 (NLT)
Don't let evil get the best of you, but conquer evil by doing good. Romans 12:21 (NLT)	Don't let evil get the best of you, but conquer evil by doing good. Romans 12:21 (NLT)

Week 8 Memory Verse

With my mouth I will greatly extol the Lord; in the great throng I will praise him. For he stands at the right hand of the needy one, to save his life from those who condemn him. Psalm 109:30-31	With my mouth I will greatly extol the Lord; in the great throng I will praise him. For he stands at the right hand of the needy one, to save his life from those who condemn him. Psalm 109:30-31
With my mouth I will greatly extol the Lord; in the great throng I will praise him. For he stands at the right hand of the needy one, to save his life from those who condemn him. Psalm 109:30-31	With my mouth I will greatly extol the Lord; in the great throng I will praise him. For he stands at the right hand of the needy one, to save his life from those who condemn him. Psalm 109:30-31
With my mouth I will greatly extol the Lord; in the great throng I will praise him. For he stands at the right hand of the needy one, to save his life from those who condemn him. Psalm 109:30-31	With my mouth I will greatly extol the Lord; in the great throng I will praise him. For he stands at the right hand of the needy one, to save his life from those who condemn him. Psalm 109:30-31

Week 9 Memory Verse

Peace I leave with you; my peace I give you. Jesus - John 14:27	Peace I leave with you; my peace I give you. Jesus - John 14:27
Peace I leave with you; my peace I give you. Jesus - John 14:27	Peace I leave with you; my peace I give you. Jesus - John 14:27
Peace I leave with you; my peace I give you. Jesus - John 14:27	Peace I leave with you; my peace I give you. Jesus - John 14:27

Week 10 Memory Verse

And we rejoice in the hope of the glory of God. Not only so, but we also rejoice in our sufferings, because we know that suffering produces perseverance; perseverance, character; and character, hope. Romans 5:2b-3	And we rejoice in the hope of the glory of God. Not only so, but we also rejoice in our sufferings, because we know that suffering produces perseverance; perseverance, character; and character, hope. Romans 5:2b-3
And we rejoice in the hope of the glory of God. Not only so, but we also rejoice in our sufferings, because we know that suffering produces perseverance; perseverance, character; and character, hope. Romans 5:2b-3	And we rejoice in the hope of the glory of God. Not only so, but we also rejoice in our sufferings, because we know that suffering produces perseverance; perseverance, character; and character, hope. Romans 5:2b-3
And we rejoice in the hope of the glory of God. Not only so, but we also rejoice in our sufferings, because we know that suffering produces perseverance; perseverance, character; and character, hope. Romans 5:2b-3	And we rejoice in the hope of the glory of God. Not only so, but we also rejoice in our sufferings, because we know that suffering produces perseverance; perseverance, character; and character, hope. Romans 5:2b-3

www.ingramcontent.com/pod-product-compliance
Lightning Source LLC
Chambersburg PA
CBHW080506110426
42742CB00017B/3014